COOKING THE GREEK WAY

UNIFORM WITH THIS VOLUME

COOKING
THE GREEK WAY

MARO DUNCAN

PAUL HAMLYN • LONDON

TO MY SON IAN

In appreciation of his helpful criticism

© *Paul Hamlyn Limited 1964*

WESTBOOK HOUSE · FULHAM BROADWAY · LONDON

Printed in Czechoslovakia

T 1306

Contents

Introduction

In a lyrical description of Greece and her beauties, the author of a well-known travel book is full of praise for Greek food and wines, because 'they are superb'. Greek food certainly is very good indeed, being both wholesome and appetizing. To most foreigners it is more palatable than Spanish and, to some, better than Italian cooking. Of course, there may be people who do not like it: perhaps those who were unfortunate in their choice of restaurant, or have never tasted real Greek home cooking or eaten at one of the better known *tavernas* where the food is the next best thing!

Greeks bring the same enthusiasm and verve to their cooking that they bring to everything they do. They are rather inclined to over-tip the oil bottle and work on the principle that if one clove of garlic improves the flavour three cloves should improve it three times as much, but this generosity can be easily remedied. I have cut down slightly on the olive oil and garlic in a few of these recipes to make it more acceptable to the foreign palate, without impairing the flavour or the authenticity of the dish.

Not all Greek recipes call for olive oil, however, for butter and margarine (in Greece it is called *phytini*) are used quite extensively now. Yet in ancient Greece butter was unknown for a long time. It was the 'Barbarian' invaders who first introduced it into the country, and even then it was used only as a kind of cold cream to rub on the body after bathing. The Greeks learned how to make it, and later finding the taste to their liking they introduced it into their diet. The Romans acquired the knowledge from the Greeks and thus the use of butter spread westwards.

Greek cooking goes back to antiquity. Homer mentions the banquets where several kinds of meats and wines were offered to the guests. In the very early days the cooks were nothing but slaves. Later, however, the cook acquired a new status, and emerged as a person of considerable importance who ruled as master over the other slaves in the household. Indeed, he must have enjoyed such importance that a proverb of that time said 'When the cook makes a mistake, it is the flute player who receives the blows.' But to become a cook the slave had to serve an apprenticeship for two years under the direction of a master chef, and also to study books which set down the rules of his art. Only after long study and hard work could he aspire to reach the top of the tree, which, incidentally, was highly lucrative!

The cook who invented a new dish was permitted, by a special law, the sole privilege of making and selling it to the public. In a book called *Deipnosofistai* ('Dinnertable philosophers') by Athenaeus, who lived in A.D. 2 one of the characters, a cook, says with some pride, 'I have earned in my profession as much as any comedian has ever earned in his own ... my art is a smoke-blackened empire'! I do not know if comedians were paid then as highly as some of them are paid nowadays, but the inference is obvious.

Much of the brilliant gastronomic literature of these times was lost by the burning of the library in Alexandria and only the names of the authors still remain. One book by the philosopher Archestratus, who lived about 330 B.C., might very well be the oldest gastronomic book known. In it, Archestratus wrote not only about food and cooking, but having travelled widely in search of foreign delicacies for the table he recorded also the eating habits and customs of other people. A number of Greek cooks left illustrious names behind them in other spheres. Cadmus, for instance, who founded ancient Thebes and introduced the alphabet into Greece, was an assistant-cook to the King of Sidon. Aesop, famous for his fables, was a slave and had to do the cooking in his master's household.

Practically all the vegetables known to the modern world were known to the Greeks, with the exception of the potato and the tomato. Everything was cooked in the most elaborate way with a multitude of herbs, oils and seasonings, or served with a rich sauce. In fact, some of the sauces which are universally used to this day date back to Greece. It was Orion who invented white sauce, and brown sauce was concocted by Lampriadis, another of the celebrated cooks of the Golden Era. It was the Greek cooks who invented pastry, though one must admit that the French perfected the art, and Epicurus of Athens provided us with an adjective symbolizing luxurious refinement in gastronomy.

When the Roman Empire took over from Greece in the 7th century the Romans sent a deputation to Athens to study Greek Arts and Letters, and to bring back the laws of Solon. According to Horace 'Greece conquered her uncouth victor' and taught the Romans the art of good eating. Greek cooks were sent to Rome to prepare the meals for the Emperor's banquets and to teach their culinary art. The Romans proved apt pupils, and in some respects they outdid their teachers in their search for exotic and luxurious foods. When Rome, inviolate for 800 years, fell to the Germanic tribes from the North, the art of cooking almost disappeared. Many of the famous cooks were killed, others gave up practising and some escaped to monasteries where they continued cooking under the guise of monks. In acknowledgment of their superiority they adopted the white cap, instead of wearing the black cap worn by the monks. It was only during the Renaissance that the French cuisine really came into its own, and in Britain it was William the Conqueror who brought in the great cooks.

Modern Greek cooking is not so elaborate as in ancient times. Also some foreign influence has crept in, without, however, detracting from the national characteristics. On the whole it is neither difficult nor extravagant. Most of the ingredients can be bought in large towns, particularly where there are Greek or Cypriot shops. With a few exceptions, a lot of the preparation can be done at any time of the day or even overnight and there is only the minimum amount of washing up. It can be kept waiting for late comers and reheated without fear of spoiling. There are also many dishes which will suit the bed-sitter cook who has only one gas ring or hot plate.

As in ancient Greece, herbs, oils, spices and wine are freely used in most dishes. I must admit here that wine and brandy are very much cheaper in Greece than they are in Britain, but wine need not be of the best quality and it does make a lot of difference to the dish. It enhances the flavour of good food and makes indifferent food taste delicious. Tomatoes, onions, garlic and lemons play a large part in Greek cooking, as do rice and pasta. As a matter of fact, the variety and consumption of pasta in Greece is as great as it is in Italy.

Making the most of the ingredients at her disposal the average Greek housewife is a good and thrifty cook. Instead of adhering strictly to the recipes, she uses her imagination, which perhaps accounts for the fact that the same dish can be prepared in umpteen different ways and called many different names. She gets along nicely without the many gadgets that we in the West have come to regard as such a necessary part of our kitchen. The can-opener and the deep-freeze are not her best friends — only casual acquaintances. She has, however, one great asset — a most appreciative husband. I have yet to meet the Greek who does not relish the delights of good food! Furthermore, she learns very early in life to follow the advice of the famous Roumanian queen-authoress, Carmen Sylva, who wrote, 'If you discover that your husband has no heart, don't forget that he has got a stomach!'

An artist, by combining different colours, can obtain different effects and yet still retain his own individuality and style. In the same way, although food is basically the same the world over, it is the way in which the ingredients are combined that reveals the subtle difference between the dishes of one country and another.

I do hope that you will have fun venturing into the world of Greek cooking, and that you will get as much enjoyment out of making at least some of the dishes as I have had in compiling them.

Some Useful Facts and Figures

Comparison of English and American Weights and Measurements

English weights and measures have been used throughout this book. 3 teaspoonfuls equal 1 tablespoon. The average English teacup is ¼ pint or 1 gill. The average English breakfast cup is ½ pint or 2 gills.

When cups are mentioned in recipes they refer to a B.S.I. measuring cup which holds ½ pint or 10 fluid ounces. The B.S.I. standard tablespoon measures 1 fluid ounce.

In case it is wished to translate any of the weights and measures into their American, Canadian or French counterparts, the following tables give a comparison.

Solid Measure

English	American
1 lb. Butter or other Fat	2 cups
1 lb. Flour	4 cups
1 lb. Granulated or Castor Sugar	2 cups
1 lb. Icing or Confectioners' Sugar	3 cups
1 lb. Brown (moist) Sugar	2½ cups
1 lb. Golden Syrup or Treacle	1 cup
1 lb. Rice	2 cups
1 lb. Dried Fruit	2 cups
1 lb. Chopped Meat (finely packed)	2 cups
1 lb. Lentils or Split Peas	2 cups
1 lb. Coffee (unground)	2½ cups
1 lb. Soft Breadcrumbs	4 cups
½ oz. Flour	1 level tablespoon★
1 oz. Flour	1 heaped tablespoon
1 oz. Sugar	1 level tablespoon
½ oz. Butter	1 level tablespoon smoothed off
1 oz. Golden Syrup or Treacle	1 level tablespoon
1 oz. Jam or Jelly	1 level tablespoon

★ must be proper measuring tablespoon

Liquid Measure

The most important difference to be noted is that the American and Canadian pint is 16 fluid ounces, as opposed to the British Imperial pint, which is 20 fluid ounces. The American ½-pint measuring cup is therefore actually equivalent to two-fifths of a British pint.

French Weights and Measures

It is difficult to convert to French measures with absolute accuracy, but 1 oz. is equal to approximately 30 grammes, 2 lb. 3 oz. to 1 kilogramme. For liquid measure, approximately 1¾ English pints may be regarded as equal to 1 litre; 1 demilitre is half a litre, and 1 décilitre is one-tenth of a litre.

Oven Temperatures

	Electricity °F.	Gas Regulo	°C.
COOL oven	225 to 250	0 to ½	107 to 121
VERY SLOW oven	250 to 275	½ to 1	121 to 135
SLOW oven	275 to 300	1 to 2	135 to 149
VERY MODERATE oven	300 to 350	2 to 3	149 to 177
MODERATE oven	375	4	190
MODERATELY HOT oven	400	5	204
HOT oven	425 to 450	6 to 7	218 to 233
VERY HOT oven	475 to 500	8 to 9	246 to 260

Note. This table is an approximate guide only. Different makes of cooker vary and if you are in any doubt about the setting it is as well to refer to the manufacturer's temperature chart.

Ingredients Used in Greek Cooking

Phyllo pastry

This is available in Greek and Cypriot shops everywhere and can be ordered by post. It is sold in 8-oz., 12-oz. and 16-oz. packets and there are about 25 sheets of pastry in each 1-lb. packet, measuring 12 × 16 inches. It costs a little more than commercially made puff pastry but it goes a good deal further.

Kataifi pastry

This is sold in 1-lb. packets at the same price as phyllo pastry.

Feta cheese

This is used in pies and *bourekakia* snacks, is made from ewes' milk. It is chalk-white, crumbly and has a distinctive flavour. It is a farmhouse type of cheese and very popular in Greece, where there are several varieties. It is usually imported in tubs, mostly from Cyprus. As it is sometimes inclined to be rather salty, it is advisable to rinse it in cold water before using it. A favourite Greek breakfast is sliced *feta*, brown bread, and apricot or strawberry jam.

Kasseri

This is a rich, creamy cheese suitable for eating and cooking.

Kefalotyri

This is a hard, grating cheese suitable for cooking. If unobtainable, use Parmesan or Cheddar instead.

Aniseed

This is used in bread and cake making and can be bought at any chemist's.

Sesame seeds

These are used in bread and cake making and have a toasted, nutty flavour; can be bought in most vegetarian and health shops. Sesame seed oil is the main ingredient of the commercially made *halva*.

Pine kernels and pistachio nuts

Both are used extensively in stuffings and in puddings. Pistachio nuts are also used in cakes and ice-cream making and can be bought in vegetarian shops and better-class grocers'.

Ouzo

This is the Greek aperitif *par excellence*, and is made of grapes. It tastes faintly of aniseed and goes milky when mixed with water. Sometimes it is used in baking instead of brandy. It can be bought in England.

Utensils Used in Greek Cooking

A pestle and mortar

Personally I prefer a wooden one, which costs very little and helps to make a smooth *taramosalata* and aubergine purée.

A skillet

This is the nearest substitute I can think of for the heavy-bottomed, wide and low Greek saucepan, which is used for *plaki* and *dolma* dishes. A frying pan with a lid, or any shallow covered dish which can be used on top of the stove, could be substituted.

An unglazed earthenware casserole

For dishes such as *giouvetsi*.

Hors-d'Oeuvre and Salads

To the Greek the *mezé* is a must with his drink! When he orders a glass of *ouzo*, beer or *retsina* in his favourite *taverna* or restaurant, he expects and always gets a little dish or two of these delectable appetizers as an accompaniment to his drink: enormous black olives, pickled or *au naturel*, fat prawns in mayonnaise or perhaps some grilled octopus. And what is more, the number of dishes will increase and the variety and quality improve with every subsequent glass.

You can almost have a meal for the price of 3–4 drinks, and this is no effort in the very hot summer months I can assure you! There is a great variety of hot and cold *mezédes*. The quality, of course, depends on where you take your aperitif, for the more sophisticated the place the more sophisticated you will find the *mezédes*. This applies also to private homes, where *mezédes* are served as a first course for either lunch or dinner. Dinner, as everyone who has visited Greece knows, is anything up to midnight, after the shows close. At times, these *mezédes* can be so substantial that they leave no room for the main course. However, they play an important part on the Greek menu, and if nothing else they do soak up the drink (at least that is what the Greeks claim, and it is a fact that drunkenness is rare in Greece).

Some of these *mezédes* would make excellent and unusual tit-bits for a cocktail party: and what hostess would not like to surprise her guests with something quite new in that line?

Elies tsakistes

Pickled olives

1 lb. black or green olives	bay leaves
1 lemon	thyme
peppercorns	1 tablespoon vinegar
	½ pint olive oil

Wash the olives, and put a few to cover the bottom of a 2-lb. glass jar. Add one slice of lemon, 2–3 peppercorns, ½ bay leaf and a good pinch of thyme. Continue in this fashion until all the ingredients have been used up. Pour over the olive oil and the vinegar, adding more if necessary, to cover completely. Cover the jar tightly and leave for a few days before using. The flavour improves with keeping.

Bourekakia me tyri

Bourekakia with cheese filling

Bourekakia are small pastry snacks filled with various mixtures and either baked or fried. Like a lot of other Greek recipes for pies and tarts, they call for phyllo pastry, which can be bought quite easily in Greece and other Balkan countries. It is as thin as tissue paper and although it is possible to make it at home given the required experience and the necessary long and very slim rolling pin, the finished result is nowhere near the

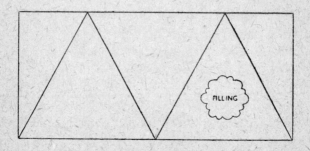

standard of the commercial product. Although the ingredients are simple enough (flour, baking powder and water), it takes a man 2–3 years to perfect this craft. The phyllo pastry can now be bought by the pound in Greek and Cypriot shops in most large towns.

Filling:

8 oz. feta or white Cheshire cheese	salt and pepper
2 egg yolks	8 oz. phyllo pastry (10–12 sheets)
1 tablespoon chopped dill or parsley	2 tablespoons melted butter

To make filling:

Soak the feta for 5 minutes. Rinse and crumble or mash with a fork. Beat the egg yolks and add them to the cheese, dill or parsley and seasoning. Be careful with the salt, because feta is usually salty enough.

To make bourekakia:

Cut the pastry in strips* 3 × 12 inches (the sheets are usually 15½- × 12-inches). Stack them one on top of the other to prevent them from drying, as they become brittle and difficult to handle. Brush each strip with melted butter, put one teaspoon of the filling on one end and roll up like a Swiss roll. Arrange on a greased baking tray and brush each roll with melted butter. They should be the thickness of a fat cigar. Bake in a moderate oven for 15–20 minutes, or until golden brown.

* Variation:

You can cut the pastry to make little triangles (see diagram) and deep fry them in oil or butter, until golden brown. There is no need to brush with butter if they are to be fried, but see that the end is tucked between the folds to prevent it from coming apart when frying.

Bourekakia me loukanika

Bourekakia with frankfurters

4 SERVINGS

5 tablespoons butter
4 level tablespoons flour
¼ pint hot milk
salt and pepper

1 egg yolk
2 oz. grated cheese
4 frankfurter sausages
8 oz. phyllo pastry

Melt half the butter and add the flour, stirring over gentle heat until well blended. Gradually add the hot milk and simmer for 5–6 minutes until the sauce is thick and creamy. Remove from heat, season to taste and stir in the cheese and egg yolk. Skin the frankfurters and cut into very small pieces. Add to the sauce and mix thoroughly. Make the bourekakia (see above). Brush over with rest of melted butter and bake in a moderate oven for 15–20 minutes. Serve hot.

Bourekakia me myala

Bourekakia with brains filling

4 SERVINGS

8 oz. phyllo pastry

Filling:

2 sets sheeps' brains
1 tablespoon vinegar
2 tablespoons flour
1 tablespoon grated cheese

2 eggs
salt and pepper
nutmeg, to taste

Soak the brains in tepid water for about 10 minutes. Remove as much of the membrane as possible and rinse well. Put the brains in a small saucepan, cover with water, add salt and vinegar and bring to the boil. Simmer for 10–12 minutes. Drain well, mash with a fork and add the flour, cheese, beaten eggs, nutmeg, salt and pepper. Make the bourekakia (see page 17), and bake in a moderate oven for 20 minutes.

Bourekakia me jamboni
Bourekakia with ham filling

4 SERVINGS

8 oz. phyllo pastry

Filling:

3 tablespoons butter
4 tablespoons flour
salt and pepper
½ pint milk
2 egg yolks

3 tablespoons grated cheese
6 oz. ham

Melt the butter over low heat, add the flour mixed with the seasoning and stir until well blended. Heat the milk and pour in gradually, while stirring constantly with a wooden spoon. Cook until the sauce thickens. Remove from the heat and add the beaten egg yolks, grated cheese and chopped ham. Make the bourekakia (see page 17).

Brush over with butter and bake in a moderate oven for 20 minutes. Serve hot.

Tarama keftedes

Fish roe cakes **(1)**

4–6 Servings

6 oz. cod's roe
6 oz. bread
3–4 tablespoons flour
½ level teaspoon baking
powder
1 tablespoon chopped
parsley

1 tablespoon chopped
dill
2–3 tablespoons chopped
onion
olive oil for deep
frying

Scald the roe and remove the membrane. Put in a basin and mash well. Soak the bread in water for a few minutes, squeeze dry and add to the roe. Add the flour, baking powder, parsley, dill and seasoning. Fry the chopped onion in a little oil until it becomes transparent, but not coloured, and add to the other ingredients. Mix well with a wooden spoon. Shape into flat cakes, dip in flour and deep fry in smoking hot olive oil until brown and crisp. Drain on kitchen paper and serve very hot.

Tarama keftedes

Fish roe cakes **(2)**

4–6 Servings

6–8 oz. fish roe
1 lb. potatoes
2–3 small onions
1 tablespoon olive oil
1 level tablespoon flour
2 tablespoons chopped
parsley

2 tablespoons chopped
dill
1–2 eggs
salt and pepper
oil for frying

Put the roe in a muslin bag and dip into boiling water for 5–10 minutes. Remove, peel off the membrane, put in a basin and mash well with a fork. Wash and boil the potatoes until tender. Remove skins and put through a 'mouli' grater. Combine the potatoes and roe. Grate the onions and lightly fry in the oil. Add parsley, dill and seasoning. Add to the potato mixture and beat in the eggs. Shape into flat cakes, dip in flour and fry until golden brown on both sides.

Tyropites

Cheese tartlets

4 SERVINGS

Pastry:

8 oz. plain flour
pinch salt
1 teaspoon baking powder
8 oz. butter or margarine
½ egg white
1 tablespoon water

Filling:

8 oz. grated cheese
2 egg yolks
1 tablespoon chopped
  parsley
salt and pepper

To make pastry:

Sift the flour, salt and baking powder into a basin. Cut the butter into tiny pieces and stir into the flour. Whip the egg white with the water and add to the flour mixture. Knead lightly with fingertips and roll out ⅛ inch thick. Have ready 12 greased patty tins. Cut 2 pastry rounds for each patty tin. Line patty tins with one of the rounds.

To make filling:

Beat the egg yolks with the salt and pepper and add the grated cheese and chopped parsley. Put a good teaspoonful of the filling in each tin, brush round the edges with a little egg white and place the remaining pastry rounds on top. Press down to seal the edges. Bake in a moderate oven for 20 minutes.

Tyri tiganito

Fried cheese

2 SERVINGS

1 oz. butter
4 oz. feta or gruyère
cheese

salt and pepper
lemon juice

Melt the butter in a small frying pan and add the cheese
cut into ¼-inch slices. Fry gently until the cheese starts
bubbling. Remove from the heat, add salt and pepper
and a good squeeze of lemon juice and serve at once.

Midia yemista

Stuffed mussels

6 SERVINGS

24 large mussels

Filling:

2 large onions
¼ pint olive oil
4 oz. rice, soaked
¼ pint stock or water
chopped parsley
chopped dill

2 oz. pine kernels
2 oz. currants
salt and pepper
cinnamon
lemon juice

To make filling:

Chop the onions and fry in a deep saucepan in oil until
just beginning to colour. Add the rice previously soaked
in cold water and drained and continue frying for about
15 minutes, then gradually add the stock or water and
let it simmer gently until the liquid is absorbed. Mix
in the chopped parsley, dill, pine kernels and currants
and add the seasoning to taste. Add the cinnamon and
let the mixture cool before using it. Prepare mussels.

To prepare mussels:

Scrub the mussels with a stiff brush and wash well in several waters. Open the shells with a small sharp knife, but be careful to keep them joined at the pointed end. Remove the little tail and any black parts which cling to the tail and rinse well.

To stuff mussels:

Put a spoonful of stuffing into each shell, but be careful not to overstuff, because the mixture swells in cooking, close the shells and put them tightly together in a skillet. Pour over enough water to cover them completely, add some more salt, pepper and a squeeze of lemon juice, put a plate on top to keep them from moving about and simmer until there is no liquid left in the pan, about 30–35 minutes. These can be eaten straight from the shell hot or cold, but preferably cold with slices of lemon.

Midia tiganita

Fried mussels

4–6 SERVINGS

1–2 eggs	1 lb. mussels, shelled
salt and pepper	and prepared
4 oz. flour	(see above)
¼ pint beer	lemon slices
oil for deep frying	

Beat the eggs with the salt and pepper and gradually fold in the sifted flour. Mix well. Stir in the beer and beat well for a few more minutes. Leave the batter to rest for 30–40 minutes. Get the oil smoking hot in a deep frying pan, dip the prepared mussels in the batter and fry them until golden brown. Drain on kitchen paper and serve very hot. Garnish with lemon slices. If your mussels are very small, mix them in the batter and fry them in spoonfuls.

Dolmadakia

Stuffed vine leaves

8 SERVINGS

12 oz. fresh vine leaves
or 1 15-oz. can
1 lb. onions
½ pint olive oil
8 oz. rice, soaked
½ pint boiling water
salt and pepper
1 tablespoon chopped
parsley
juice 1 large lemon

1 tablespoon chopped
dill or
1 tablespoon chopped
mint
lemon wedges
1 tablespoon currants
(optional)
1 tablespoon pine kernels
(optional)

Plunge the fresh vine leaves in boiling water for 5–10 minutes, or if canned ones are used rinse well and drain. Meanwhile prepare the stuffing. Chop the onions very fine, or grate. Heat half the olive oil in a fairly deep pan and fry the onions without letting them colour. Add the rice, previously soaked in salted water and drained, mix well and cook gently for about 20 minutes. Gradually add the boiling water, salt, pepper, chopped parsley, dill or mint, and the lemon juice. Cover tightly and simmer until all the water is absorbed, about 20 minutes. Let the mixture cool a little. Take one vine leaf, cut off the stalk and with the rough side towards you put one good teaspoon of the mixture on the widest part. Fold over and tuck the ends in. Roll up to make a neat little parcel, roughly 1 × 2 inches wide. If required for cocktail snacks, make them smaller. Continue until all the mixture is used up. Put a layer of vine leaves in a skillet and place the dolmadakia close together in rows. Pour over the rest of the olive oil and enough hot water to cover them completely. Add some more salt and pepper to taste. Put a plate on top to keep them from moving about, cover with a lid and cook over a low heat for 1 hour. Serve cold, garnished with wedges of lemon.

Note:

This is the classical recipe. If liked you can add 1 table-spoon currants and 1 tablespoon pine kernels to the mixture.

Tiganites kolokithia

Courgette fritters

4–6 SERVINGS

Batter:

6 medium-sized
   courgettes
salt
2 tablespoons olive oil
1 tablespoon lemon
   juice

5 oz. flour
¼ pint beer
1 tablespoon olive oil
salt
1 egg white
oil for deep frying

Scrape the courgettes and cut into rounds about ¼ inch thick. Sprinkle them with salt and leave them to stand for 30–35 minutes. Mix the olive oil with the lemon juice in a small basin. Dry the courgette rounds and throw them into the mixture. Leave them to soak for another 30 minutes, turning them occasionally.

In the meantime prepare the batter with the flour, beer, olive oil and a good pinch of salt. Let it stand for a while in a cool place and just before you are ready to fry add the stiffly beaten egg white. Dip the courgette rounds in the batter and deep fry until golden brown and well puffed. Drain on kitchen paper and serve at once.

Avga yemista

Stuffed eggs

4–8 SERVINGS

8 hard-boiled eggs
salt and pepper
3 tablespoons mayonnaise
(see pages 195-6)

mustard
few drops lemon juice
4 oz. prawns or crab
meat

Shell and cut the eggs in half lengthwise. Scoop out the yolks and mash them with the seasoning, mayonnaise, mustard and lemon juice. Add the finely chopped prawns or crab meat and mix well. Place the halves of egg white on a flat dish and stuff them with the mixture. Place half a prawn on top to decorate. Serve cold.

Salingaria

Snails

4 SERVINGS

24 snails
3–4 tablespoons olive oil
1 large chopped onion
1 clove garlic

3–4 peeled tomatoes
1 tablespoon chopped
parsley
salt and pepper

Prepare snails by putting in a basin and covering with water, or in a bag of bran. Leave overnight. Rinse thoroughly and cover with fresh water. Boil the snails for 30 minutes, remove from the pan and place in a collander. Rinse under running water. In the meantime, heat the olive oil in a skillet and lightly fry the onion and crushed garlic. Press the tomatoes through a strainer and add to the onions with the parsley, salt and pepper and ¼ pint hot water. Simmer for 5 minutes and add the snails. Cover with a lid and cook gently for a further

30 minutes. If preferred, the snails can be removed from their shells and cooked for a shorter time. The same applies to canned snails.

Soufflé me tyri

Mock cheese soufflé

4 SERVINGS

1 small loaf bread
4 oz. butter or margarine, softened
8 oz. gruyère cheese
3 slices ham
8 oz. kasseri or Parmesan cheese
4 eggs
1 pint milk
salt and pepper

Butter thin slices of bread on both sides. Grease a soufflé dish and line with the bread slices. Cover with slices of gruyère and place the ham on top. Sprinkle thickly with the grated cheese. Beat the eggs with the milk and seasoning and carefully pour over the dish. Allow to stand for 30 minutes and bake in a moderate oven for about 1 hour, or until the top is firm and golden brown.

Pandzaria sauté

Beetroot sauté

3 tablespoons olive oil
1 chopped onion
1 clove garlic
6–8 cooked beetroots
1 tablespoon flour
1 tablespoon wine vinegar
salt and pepper
1 tablespoon chopped parsley

Heat the olive oil in a small pan and fry the onion and garlic until golden brown. Add the diced beetroot and cook for 1–2 minutes. Sprinkle in the flour, salt and pepper and gradually stir in the vinegar. Add the chopped parsley, cover the pan with a lid and cook gently for 10 minutes.

Tyropitakia

Small cheese turnovers

4 oz. melted butter
4 oz. grated feta
  cheese

6 oz. flour
  (approximately)
pinch salt

Sieve the flour into a basin, make a well in the middle
and add the melted but not hot butter and the cheese,
and salt if needed. Sometime the feta is salt enough on
its own. Mix thoroughly to make a soft dough. Leave
in the refrigerator for at least 3 hours. Take nut-sized
pieces and flatten between your palms to form rounds
about ⅛ inch thick. Fold the rounds in two and bake
in a moderate oven for 15 minutes. These are usually
served hot as an accompaniment to auzo or beer.

Spetsofagi

Sausages with green peppers

4 SERVINGS

4–5 tablespoons olive oil
4 large green peppers
1 lb. tomatoes
  (or medium-sized tin)

2 cloves garlic
salt
cooked frankfurters,
  sausages or liver

Heat the oil in a saucepan and fry the deseeded and finely
sliced peppers. Peel and slice the tomatoes and add to
the peppers. Simmer covered for 20–30 minutes until
a thick pulp. Add the finely chopped garlic, salt and
sausages or liver cut into small pieces. Cook for a further
10 minutes. Serve very hot.

Patates moussaka

Potato moussaka

4–6 SERVINGS

2 lb. potatoes
2 oz. butter or
    margarine
12 oz. minced beef
2 finely chopped onions
2 tablespoons flour
$\frac{1}{4}$ pint wine
3–4 peeled chopped
    tomatoes

1 tablespoon chopped
    parsley
salt and pepper
2 stiffly beaten egg
    whites
3 tablespoons toasted
    breadcrumbs
2 egg yolks
$\frac{1}{3}$ pint milk

Peel and cut the potatoes into $\frac{1}{4}$-inch thick slices and fry lightly. Heat the butter in a saucepan and fry the minced meat and onions. Sprinkle in 1 oz. of the flour and cook until nicely brown. Add the wine, tomatoes, parsley, and seasoning, cover the pan and cook for 20 minutes. Remove from the heat, cool slightly and fold in the stiffly beaten egg whites. Sprinkle the bottom of a greased casserole with breadcrumbs and arrange a layer of potatoes, cover with a layer of meat and continue filling the dish in this way, finishing with a layer of potatoes. Cover the casserole and place in a moderate oven for 30 minutes. Beat the egg yolks and stir in the other tablespoon of flour and milk with a pinch of salt and pepper. Pour this mixture on top of the potatoes and return to the oven uncovered to cook until firm and lightly brown.

Piperies salata

Green pepper salad

4 SERVINGS

4 medium-sized green
  peppers
3 tablespoons olive oil

2 tablespoons wine
  vinegar
salt and pepper

Place the peppers under the grill and cook until the
skin cracks. Peel off the skin and remove the seeds. Slice
thinly, season and cover with a mixture of oil and vinegar.
Chill and serve.

Piperies yemistes salata

Stuffed green pepper salad

4 SERVINGS

For garnish:

4 medium-sized green
  peppers
6 oz. myzithra or cottage
  cheese
1 finely chopped spring
  onion
3–4 finely chopped green
  olives
2 teaspoons chopped
  watercress
3 teaspoons mayonnaise
  (see pages 195-6)
salt and pepper

tomatoes
cucumber
watercress

Cut off the top of the peppers and remove the seeds
and membrane. Mash the myzithra, or cottage cheese,
with the spring onion, olives and chopped watercress,
and bind with the mayonnaise. Season well and stuff
the peppers with this mixture. Leave in a refrigerator

for a few hours. When ready to serve, cut into $\frac{1}{2}$-inch slices and serve on a platter garnished with sliced tomatoes, cucumber and sprigs of watercress.

Melidzanes salata

Aubergine salad (1)

4–6 SERVINGS

4 medium-sized aubergines	1 tablespoon chopped parsley
$\frac{1}{4}$ pint olive oil	salt and pepper
1 tablespoon lemon juice	1 tablespoon grated onion

Select dark purple aubergines with firm smooth skins. Bake or grill until the skin turns brown and blisters. As soon as the aubergines are cool enough to handle remove the stalk and peel off the burned skin. Put on a chopping board and while still warm cut up the creamy flesh (preferably with a stainless steel or wooden chopping knife, because metal blackens the aubergines) into very small pieces. Place in a bowl and mash well, adding the oil drop by drop and a little lemon juice. When wel blended mix in the rest of tqe oil, lemon juice, chopped parsley and seasoning to taste , stirring all the time with a wooden spon. Add the grated onion just before serwing. Serve cold.

Though the Greeks calt it a salad, strictly speaking this is a purée and it is delicious served with cold meats, or cold roast chicken.

Melidzanosalata

Aubergine salad (2)

2–4 SERVINGS

2 medium-sized
aubergines
juice 1 lemon
2 hard-boiled eggs,
finely chopped
3–4 tablespoons diced
cucumber

2 cloves garlic,
crushed
seasoning
3–4 tablespoons
mayonnaise
(see pages 195-6)

Bake the aubergines in a hot oven for 30 minutes. Remove the brown, blistered skin and put the flesh on to a board. Chop very finely and place in a bowl. Squeeze in the lemon juice and add the eggs, cucumber, crushed garlic and seasoning. Bind with the mayonnaise. Chill well and serve with crisp French bread or cream crackers.

Anginares salata

Artichoke salad

4 SERVINGS

6 large globe
artichokes
½ lemon
6 tablespoons olive
oil

2 tablespoons lemon juice
or 2–3 tablespoons
thin mayonnaise
(see pages 195-6)
salt and pepper

Prepare the artichokes as for Artichokes in Oil (see page 171). Cook covered in boiling salted water, to which you have added 1 teaspoon lemon juice and a strip of lemon rind, for 30–45 minutes or until tender. Remove artichokes with a perforated spoon and drain thoroughly before putting in the salad bowl. Serve either with a mixture of oil and lemon or thin mayonnaise.

Tarama salata

Fish roe salad

Tarama is the roe of the grey mullet, but as this is difficult to obtain outside Greece smoked cod's roe is a very good alternative.

4 SERVINGS

4 oz. smoked cod's roe	1 tablespoon water
2 oz. stale bread, soaked	little grated onion
¼ pint olive oil	(optional)
juice 2 lemons	chopped parsley

Soak bread in water. Remove the skin from the roe. The easiest way is to scrape the roe with a small teaspoon. Put it in a mortar and pound until smooth. Squeeze the bread dry, add to the roe and continue pounding until well blended. Gradually add the olive oil and the lemon juice, and beat either with a fork or a wire whisk until all the liquid is absorbed and the mixture is a smooth paste. Add the tablespoon of water and beat again. This makes it light and creamy. Finally add the finely grated onion, if used, previously washed in cold water to remove the strong smell, and some chopped parsley. This dish is an aperitif, but can also be used as a first course to a meal or as a savoury. It would also make lovely canapés for a cocktail party.

Salata psari me yaourti

Fish salad with yoghurt sauce

4 SERVINGS

1½ lb. steamed fish

Sauce:

salt and pepper
4-5 tablespoons mayonnaise
  sauce (see pages 195-6)

1 jar yoghurt
1 tablespoon chopped
  spring onion
1 tablespoon capers
1 tablespoon chopped dill
2 hard-boiled eggs

Shred the cooked fish and put into a salad bowl. Season well. Mix the mayonnaise sauce with the yoghurt. Add the chopped onion and capers and pour over the fish. Decorate with chopped dill and slices of hard-boiled eggs.

Angourosalata me yaourti

Cucumber salad with yoghurt

4 SERVINGS

1 medium-sized cucumber

Sauce:

1 clove garlic
1 tablespoon salt

1 tablespoon white
  vinegar
1 jar yoghurt
1 tablespoon olive oil
1 tablespoon chopped
  dill

Crush the garlic. Add the salt and vinegar and mix to a smooth paste. Stir this into the yoghurt, add the oil and half the chopped dill. Peel and slice the cucumber, put into a salad bowl and sprinkle with a little salt. Cover with the yoghurt sauce and sprinkle the rest of the dill on top. Chill well before serving.

Fassolakia salata

French bean salad

4 SERVINGS

1½ lb. French beans
2 tablespoons finely
  chopped parsley
2 cloves garlic

5 tablespoons olive oil
2 tablespoons vinegar
salt and pepper

Choose young small beans. String and cut them in two.
Drop into boiling salted water and cook until tender.
Drain and place in a salad bowl. Mix the oil, vinegar,
sliced garlic and parsley, and pour over the beans. Blend
thoroughly and serve well chilled.

Fassolia salata

Haricot bean salad

4 SERVINGS

8 oz. haricot beans
3 tablespoons olive oil
1 tablespoon vinegar
salt and pepper
1 tablespoon chopped
  onion

1 tablespoon chopped
  parsley
1 tablespoon chopped
  green pepper

Soak the beans overnight. Rinse and put them to boil
in fresh cold water until tender. Do not add salt until
they are almost cooked. When ready, drain them well
and while still hot mix in the oil, vinegar and seasoning.
Stir well and add the chopped onion, parsley and slivers
of green pepper. Serve cold.

Soups

The purpose of soup is to induce the flow of the gastric juices and stimulate rather than satisfy the appetite. You will find, however, that many of the soups in this book are substantial enough to satisfy even good-sized appetites. As a matter of fact, in some of the Greek villages where meat is scarce and expensive a bowl of thick soup, a few olives and a chunk of brown bread make the main meal of the day. The Greeks are fond of soups and they have quite a variety of them. There are meat soups and fish soups, the Easter *mayeritsa* and the *avgolemono* soups, which must surely rate among the most delicious in any country. Pulse soups are very popular too, especially during Lent, and the thick bean soup — the *fassolada* — is undoubtedly the national dish of Greece. The sophisticated town housewife likes to serve it sieved and with croûtons, but in the traditional *fassolada* the beans are left whole: they must be very tender, of course, and the oil of the best quality. Tripe soup is also a great favourite, and it is supposed to help a hangover.

Soupa Hristouyeniatiki

Christmas soup

6–8 SERVINGS

1 lb. stewing beef	3 stalks parsley
giblets and feet from	salt and peppercorns
1 turkey	4 oz. vermicelli
2 quarts water	nut butter
2 carrots	2 egg yolks
1 onion	1 large lemon
3 stalks celery	

Put the meat, giblets and water in a large saucepan and bring to the boil. Skim well and add the chopped vegetables, salt and peppercorns. Cover the pan and simmer gently for about 2 hours. Remove meat and giblets on to a dish and keep warm. Strain the stock and return to the pan. Bring to the boil and throw in the vermicelli. Cook uncovered for 4–5 minutes and remove from the heat. Stir in the butter. Beat the egg yolks with the lemon juice and gradually add 3–4 tablespoons of the hot soup, beating constantly. Add the mixture to the remaining soup, stirring vigorously as you do so. Return the pan to the heat, but do not allow the contents to boil. Serve very hot, with tiny pieces of the giblets and some of the meat added to each bowl.

Mayeritsa

Easter soup

This is the traditional Easter soup, which is served to the family to break their fast when they return home after attending Midnight Mass on the Holy Saturday. Presumably, it was invented in order to use up the offal and other edible parts of the Pascal lamb, which is to be roasted on the Sunday.

There are several versions of this delicious and nourishing soup, and the proportions of the offal used can be varied at the discretion of the cook.

8 SERVINGS

liver, heart, tripe, entrails, lights and feet of 1 lamb
2 oz. butter
2 tablespoons chopped dill
2 tablespoons chopped parsley
1–2 tablespoons milk or thin cream
5–6 spring onions
2 eggs
2 lemons
8 tablespoons rice
salt and pepper

Thoroughly clean the tripe and feet. Put in a large saucepan, cover with water and bring to the boil. Throw this water away. Cut up the tripe and meat from the feet into small pieces and return to the saucepan. Mix flour with the water into a paste. Pour plenty of hot water over the meat, add salt and the flour paste. Place saucepan over low heat and cook gently for 30–40 minutes. In the meantime, wash a few of the intestines. Turn them inside out or slit them with scissors, and rub them with a cut lemon. Wash a piece of liver, heart and a very small piece of lung and throw them all together in a pan of boiling salted water. Boil for 5–6 minutes, remove, drain well and cut up finely. Melt the butter in a frying pan, add the chopped onions (green part included), liver, intestines and heart. Add the chopped parsley and dill, and season to taste. Cook gently for a few minutes, stirring occasionally with a wooden spoon. Mix this with the tripe and feet soup in the large saucepan and continue cooking over low heat until all the meats are tender. Strain through a sieve and return soup to the saucepan. Bring to the boil again and add the rice, previously washed in warm water. Cook until tender. Beat the egg yolks with one tablespoon cold water, add 2–3 tablespoons lemon juice, beating all the while, and about 4 tablespoons from the hot soup. Pour the egg and lemon mixture into the large saucepan, stirring vigorously, but do not allow to boil once the eggs have been added. Just before serving add the milk or cream, if used. The soup should be creamy in appearance and texture.

Kotosoupa avgolemono

Chicken soup with egg and lemon

6–8 SERVINGS

3 pints chicken stock
7–8 tablespoons pasta
   (vermicelli or fancy
   shapes)

Sauce:

2 egg yolks
3 tablespoons lemon juice
salt and pepper
knob butter or
   1 tablespoon thin
   cream

Bring the chicken stock to the boil. Add the pasta and cook uncovered until tender, but not mushy. Beat the egg yolks with the lemon juice and very gradually add 3–4 tablespoons of the soup, beating all the time. Remove the saucepan from the heat and pour in the egg and lemon mixture, stirring vigorously. Never allow the soup to boil after the egg mixture has been added. Just before serving add the knob of butter or thin cream. Serve hot.

Soupa Arapiki

Arab soup

8 SERVINGS

1 3-lb. breast of lamb
2 pints water
1 lb. onions
2 oz. butter
1 lb. fresh tomatoes

salt and pepper
1 tablespoon chopped
    mint
4 oz. pasta (star-shaped)

Put the meat in the water in a large saucepan and bring to the boil. Skim well. Slice the onions very finely and sauté them in the butter. Skin and chop the tomatoes finely. Add the onions and tomatoes to the meat. Add the salt, pepper and chopped mint. Cover and simmer gently for 2 hours. Place the meat on a hot dish and cut it up very small. Keep hot. Add the pasta to the stock and boil until tender, 5–7 minutes. Put a few pieces of meat in each individual bowl and pour the soup over it. Serve very hot.

Psarosoupa avgolemono

Fish soup with egg and lemon sauce

6 SERVINGS

2 lb. any large fish
2 onions
2–3 carrots
2–3 stalks celery
3–4 stalks parsley
2–3 potatoes
3½ pints water
4 tablespoons olive
    oil

1 tablespoon dry white
    wine
½ bay leaf
salt and pepper
1 cod's head
    (if available)
4 tablespoons rice
Egg and lemon sauce
    (see page 194)

Wash the fish and cut into suitable pieces for serving. Salt well and put aside. Peel, wash and cut the flavouring vegetables in thick slices. Put in a large saucepan and cover with the water, oil and wine. Add the parsley, bay leaf and seasoning. Bring to the boil and cook steadily until the vegetables are tender. Add the fish and the cod's head (if used) and cook very, very slowly, to avoid breaking the fish, for 12–25 minutes according to the size and quality of the fish. Strain the stock and return to the saucepan. Bring to the boil and toss in the rice. Cook until tender. Beat the egg yolks with the lemon juice and very gradually add 3–4 tablespoons of the soup, beating all the time. Remove the saucepan from the heat and pour in the egg and lemon mixture, stirring vigorously. Do not allow the soup to boil after the egg mixture has been added.

The fish and vegetables can be served with any suitable sauce or made into a fish pie.

Psarosoupa me domates

Fish soup with tomatoes

4 SERVINGS

1½ lb. cod (haddock, gurnet)	salt and pepper
2 small onions	12 oz. fresh ripe tomatoes
2 small carrots	8 tablespoons olive oil
2 stalks celery	4 tablespoons rice
3 pints water	

Clean and wash the fish, sprinkle with salt and leave in a collander to drain. Put the onions, carrots and celery in a saucepan, cover with the water and add seasoning to taste. Boil for a few minutes and add the peeled tomatoes. Simmer for 40–45 minutes and lower in the fish. Add the olive oil and cook very gently until the fish is tender. Place the fish on a hot dish and keep warm. Strain the stock back in the pan and bring to the boil. Allow 1 tablespoon of rice per person, and adjust the seasoning and cook until the rice is quite soft.

Kakavia

Fish soup

6–8 SERVINGS

1½ lb. assorted large fish (e.g. brill, bream, gurnet)
1½ lb. assorted small fish
¼ pint olive oil
1½ lb. chopped onions
3 cloves crushed garlic
3–4 tomatoes
4 pints water or fish stock
salt and pepper
1 bay leaf
1 tablespoon parsley
slices toast

Wash large fish and cut into neat portions. Rub with salt and leave aside. Remove heads and tails of small fish, clean and wash thoroughly. Salt and leave aside. Put the olive oil in a large saucepan, add the onion, garlic and sliced tomatoes, and simmer for a few minutes. Cover with the water, season well and cook gently for 30–35 minutes until the vegetables are quite tender. Throw in the small fish and continue cooking for a further 10–15 minutes. Press through a sieve and return to the pan. Bring to the boil, add the portions of fish, the bay leaf and chopped parsley, lower the heat and simmer very gently until cooked, about 20 minutes. Add the wine. Put one slice of toast in each individual bowl and a portion of the fish, and pour the thick soup over it.

Note:

Though the French may not like to admit it, the classical *bouillabaisse* is based on this humble fisherman's soup, which was first introduced to Marseilles by the Greeks in the seventh century. The French gastronomic genius perfected and glamorised it.

Soupa fava

Dried broad bean soup

6 SERVINGS

8 oz. dried broad beans
3 pints water
4 small coarsely chopped
  onions

4 tablespoons olive oil
salt and pepper
thyme or mint
fried croûtons

Soak the broad beans for 15 hours and cut off the ends.
Put in a large saucepan, cover with the water and bring
to the boil. Skim well and add the onion, olive oil and
seasoning. Simmer until the beans are very tender. Press
through a sieve and return to the pan to heat through.
Sprinkle some thyme or mint on top and serve with
crisp croûtons.

Tahinosoupa

Soup with tahini

Tahini is made from sesame seeds. If this is unobtainable
peanut butter can be used in its place.

4–6 SERVINGS

2 pints water
4 tablespoons rice
  or small pasta
4 tablespoons tahini
  or peanut butter

salt and pepper
2 tablespoons lemon
  juice

Bring the water with salt to the boil and throw in the
rice or pasta. Cook until tender. Dilute the tahini with
a little water and beat well for a few minutes, adding
a little salt, pepper and the lemon juice. While still
beating add 3–4 tablespoons from the soup and return
the mixture to the pan, stirring vigorously. The soup
should be thick and creamy.

Soupa prassa

Leek soup

4–6 SERVINGS

3 large leeks
1 oz. butter
1 chopped onion
1½ pints meat stock

1 bay leaf
3 cloves
2 large potatoes
salt and pepper

Clean and slice the leeks finely. Heat the butter in a large saucepan, and sauté the leeks and onion for 10 minutes. Add the stock, bay leaf, cloves and potatoes cut into small cubes and season well. Cover the pan with a lid and cook gently for 20 minutes.

Fakosoupa

Green lentil soup

4–6 SERVINGS

1 lb. green lentils
3 pints hot water
1 large onion
1 clove garlic
3 peeled tomatoes
2–3 carrots

1 bay leaf
2 sticks celery
1 sprig rosemary
4 tablespoons olive oil
salt and pepper
2–3 slices stale bread

Soak the lentils overnight. Rinse, put in a large pan with plenty of water and boil for 2–3 minutes. Throw away this water, return the lentils to the pan, add the hot water and the finely chopped vegetables and simmer covered until very soft. Discard the bay leaf and rosemary and rub the rest through a sieve. Return the purée to the pan, add seasoning to taste and stir in the olive oil. Fry cubes of stale bread in hot fat or oil until golden, and drain on kitchen paper. Bring soup to the boil and serve with croûtons.

Patatosoupa

Potato soup

4–6 SERVINGS

1½ lb. potatoes
3 onions
2 pints meat stock
   or water
¼ pint hot milk

2 tablespoons butter
salt and pepper
chopped parsley or
   mint

Peel and cut the potatoes and onions, and cook in the meat stock until soft. Rub through a sieve and return the purée to the pan. Add the hot milk and butter and season to taste. Reheat, and just before serving sprinkle with the parsley or mint.

Domatosoupa fides

Tomato and vermicelli soup

6–8 SERVINGS

1 lb. fresh ripe tomatoes
4 pints water
4–6 oz. vermicelli

salt and pepper
4 tablespoons butter

Force the sliced tomatoes through a sieve and put them to boil with the water for 20–25 minutes. Throw in the vermicelli, add seasoning to taste and simmer gently until the vermicelli is tender. This takes about 5 minutes. Remove from the heat and stir in the butter.

Spanakosoupa

Spinach soup

6 SERVINGS

2 lb. spinach
4 tablespoons butter
8 oz. onions
1½ pints veal or chicken stock

2 tablespoons flour
¼ pint milk
salt and pepper
nutmeg

Wash the spinach thoroughly and chop finely. Melt the butter in a saucepan, add the chopped onions and fry for a few minutes, but do not let them colour. Drain and add the spinach and continue cooking for 5–10 minutes longer. Gradually add the stock and simmer until the spinach is cooked. Press through a sieve and return to the pan. Mix the flour with the milk and pour into the soup. Season and add nutmeg. Stir and cook gently until it thickens slightly.

Revithia soupa

Chick-pea soup

6 SERVINGS

1 lb. chick-peas
pinch bicarbonate of soda
4 pints water
8 oz. onions
2 cloves garlic
5 tablespoons olive oil

salt and pepper
3 tomatoes (fresh or canned)
2 teaspoons flour
little water
1 tablespoon chopped parsley

Soak the chick-peas overnight in water in which you have dissolved a good pinch of bicarbonate of soda. Rinse well, cover with fresh water and bring quickly to the boil. Pour away this water. Put the chick-peas in a large napkin or tea towel, and rub back and forth to get rid of the skins. Rinse under the cold water tap, when the skins will float away. Return to the saucepan, cover with 4 pints of water and add the onions and garlic chopped finely, also the oil and the seasoning. Skin the tomatoes and cut into small pieces. Add to the saucepan and cook very gently until the chick-peas are very tender (3–4 hours). Mix the flour to a paste with a little water and add to the chick-peas with the chopped parsley. Stir and cook for a further 10 minutes.

Soupa me Xinithra

Sorrel soup

8 SERVINGS

4 level tablespoons butter	salt and pepper
5 level tablespoons flour	2 handfuls sorrel
4 pints meat stock, or	1 egg yolk
half milk and half meat	2 tablespoons milk
stock	nutmeg

Melt the butter in a large saucepan and gradually add the flour, stirring constantly with a wooden spoon or a wire whisk. Pour in the stock, a little at a time and stir until well blended. Season. Bring slowly to the boil, lower the heat and let it simmer for 5–10 minutes. In the meantime, pick the sorrel leaves, wash thoroughly and cut into very fine strips. This is easier with a pair of kitchen scissors. Have ready a saucepan with boiling water, plunge in the sorrel leaves and bring to the boil once. Drain well and add to the soup. Allow to simmer for 5–6 minutes. Remove from the heat and add the egg yolk previously mixed with the milk and a little more salt and pepper. Sprinkle with the nutmeg just before serving.

Soupa domata

Tomato soup

6–8 SERVINGS

2 lb. ripe tomatoes
2 pints water
4 tablespoons semolina
3 tablespoons olive oil

salt and pepper
1 teaspoon sugar
2–3 slices stale bread

Wash the tomatoes, put in a large saucepan with the water and simmer until tender. Press through a sieve and return to the pan. If the pulp is too thick add a little more water. Bring to the boil and sprinkle in the semolina. Add the oil, salt, pepper and sugar, and simmer for 15 minutes. Make croûtons by cubing some stale bread and frying until crisp and golden. Allow 1 tablespoon of croûtons per person and pour the soup over them.

Soupa domata me rizi

Tomato soup with rice

4–6 SERVINGS

1 pint water
1 pint tomato juice
3 tablespoons olive oil

salt and pepper
1 teaspoon sugar
2–3 tablespoons rice

Mix water and tomato juice and bring to the boil. Add the olive oil, salt, pepper and sugar, and sprinkle the rice. Bring to the boil again and cook gently for 15–20 minutes.

Soupa Fassolia

Bean soup

4 SERVINGS

1 lb. haricot beans
2 chopped onions
2 carrots
2 sticks celery
2–3 sprigs parsley
2 cloves garlic

2 tablespoons tomato
   purée
little water
4 tablespoons olive oil
salt and pepper
1 tablespoon flour

Soak the beans overnight. Rinse and put in a pan with fresh water and the vegetables chopped up in small dice. Bring to the boil, lower the heat and cook for 30–40 minutes. Add the tomato purée diluted in a little water, the olive oil and seasoning. Simmer until the beans are very tender. Dilute the flour in a little water and add to the contents of the pan. Boil for a further 10 minutes.

Soupa Kremydi

Onion soup

4–6 SERVINGS

5–6 tablespoons chopped
   onion
4–5 tablespoons butter
3 pints hot water or stock

salt and pepper
4 oz. grated cheese
2 slices stale bread

In a deep saucepan fry the chopped onion in butter until pale brown. Strain excess butter and keep to fry the bread in later. Add the hot water or stock to the onions, season well and simmer over low heat for about 30 minutes. In the meantime cut the bread into tiny dice and fry in the onion-flavoured butter until crisp. Put the bread in the soup bowls, cover thickly with the grated cheese and fill up with the soup. Serve very hot.

Soupa fassolakia prasina

Green bean soup

4–6 SERVINGS

1 lb. French or runner
  beans
3 oz. butter
2 finely chopped onions
2 finely chopped carrots

2½ pints stock
salt and pepper
1 tablespoon chopped
  parsley
2 oz. flour

Wash, string and cut the beans into small pieces. Heat
2 oz. of the butter in a large saucepan and lightly fry
the onions. Add the carrots and beans, cover the pan
and sauté for 5–6 minutes, shaking the pan occasionally.
Pour in 2 pints stock, seasoning and chopped parsley.
Cover and simmer until the vegetables are very tender.
Rub through a sieve and return to the pan. In the meantime, heat the rest of the butter and stir in the flour.
When well blended add the rest of the hot stock and
season lightly. Cook over low heat for 5 minutes and
pour into the vegetable purée. Stir thoroughly and serve
immediately. If the soup is too thick, add a few spoonfuls
of hot stock.

Rizosoupa Krema

Creamed rice soup

5–6 SERVINGS

2½ pints meat stock
8 oz. rice
salt and white pepper
3 egg yolks

2 oz. butter
½ pint hot milk
3–4 slices stale bread

Bring the stock to the boil, toss in the rice and cook
gently until very tender. Rub through a sieve and return
to the pan. Season to taste. Beat the egg yolks and

gradually add the hot milk, beating continuously. Stir the mixture into the rice and add the butter cut into small pieces. Stir vigorously until well blended. Fry cubed bread until golden, and serve with the hot soup.

Soupa lahano

Cabbage soup

6–8 SERVINGS

4 tablespoons butter
4 tablespoons chopped
  onion
3 pints water
1 lb. shredded white
  cabbage
1 tablespoon chopped
  parsley

1 teaspoon chopped
  dill
salt and pepper
slices of stale bread
butter for frying
cayenne

Melt the butter in a saucepan and fry the onion until nicely brown. Pour in the water and bring to the boil. Wash and shred the cabbage finely and add to the saucepan. Bring to the boil again and add the chopped dill and parsley, and season to taste. Lower the heat and cook until the cabbage is very tender.

Cut some stale bread into neat cubes and fry in hot butter until golden brown. Drain and put one tablespoonful in each individual bowl. Pour the hot soup over and sprinkle with cayenne.

Fish Dishes

In a country surrounded by the sea, it is natural that sea-food should play an important part in the diet of the people. Greece has a great variety and the quality is excellent, but the first requisite for a good fish dish is freshness and, of course, careful cooking. No matter how excellent the fish may be, the cook can make or ruin it through carelessness or lack of imagination. A little lemon juice sprinkled on the fish, to keep the flesh white and firm, before plunging it in a simmering *court-bouillon*; a little olive oil and lemon juice brushed on top before putting under the grill; a crisp light batter and careful draining before serving fried fish; these tips take only a minute or two but make the world of difference even to the most uninteresting variety.

Some of the fish mentioned in these recipes may not always be obtainable, but there is no reason

why the method of cooking could not
be applied to a similar fish. It would
make a pleasant change.

Psari me patates

Fish with potatoes

4 SERVINGS

1½ lb. any large fish	1 lb. whole small
salt and pepper	potatoes
2 chopped onion	4 tablespoons olive oil
2 sliceds carots	¼ pint water
2 sticks celery	juice 1 large lemon

Wash the fish and cut into neat portions. Sprinkle with
salt and leave in a collander to drain. Put the vegetables
in a pan and cover with the oil and water. Season well,
cover with a lid and simmer for 15 minutes. Place the
fish portions on the vegetables, pour in the lemon juice
and lower the heat as much as possible. Cook for 15–20
minutes.

Psari me saltsa elies

Grilled fish with olives

4 SERVINGS

2 lb. fish suitable for grilling
6 tablespoons olive oil
1 sliced onion
5 sliced peeled tomatoes

6 tablespoons beer
10–12 stuffed green olives
salt and pepper
lemon slices

Clean and wash the fish and leave in a collander to drain. Heat 5 tablespoons oil and fry the onion slices until golden brown. Add the tomatoes, beer, sliced olives and salt and pepper to taste. Simmer for 30 minutes. Brush the fish with the remaining oil and grill for 5–15 minutes, according to kind and thickness of fish. Put on a hot plate and pour the sauce over it. Garnish with lemon slices.

Psari marinato

Marinated fish

4 SERVINGS

4 red or grey mullet
salt and pepper
juice 1 lemon
4 level tablespoons flour
olive oil for shallow frying
4 tablespoons vinegar

8 tablespoons water
2 tablespoons tomato purée
1–2 cloves garlic
pinch sugar
2 sprigs rosemary

Clean and wash the fish. Sprinkle with salt and lemon juice, dip in the flour and shallow fry in smoking hot olive oil. Drain and place the fish on a dish and if necessary add a little more oil to the pan. Add the rest of the flour and stir with a wooden spoon until the flour turns brown. Gradually pour in the vinegar, the water in which you have first diluted the tomato purée, the crushed garlic, seasoning, sugar and rosemary. Cover the pan and let the sauce simmer for 10–15 minutes. Strain the sauce over the fish. It should be thick enough to coat the fish. This dish is usually served cold, but it is equally good eaten hot. Fish prepared in this way can be kept for 2–3 days in a cool place, provided it is completely covered by the sauce.

The Romans used to preserve fried fish in vinegar and I presume this method is based on the same principle.

Fileta psariou tiganita

Fried fish fillets

6 SERVINGS

6 fish fillets
1 tablespoon white wine
juice ½ lemon
salt and pepper

Batter:

4 oz. sifted flour
2 egg yolks
salt and pepper
2–3 tablespoons white wine
1 egg white
lemon wedges to garnish

deep olive oil for frying

Wash the fillets and put on a plate. Pour over the wine and lemon juice and sprinkle with salt and pepper. Leave them to marinate for a few minutes while you prepare the batter.

Sift the flour in a basin, make a well in the middle and add the egg yolks, salt and pepper. Pour in the wine gradually and mix well with a wooden spoon. If the mixture is too stiff add a very little water. Beat the white of egg until stiff and fold in carefully into the mixture. Drain the fillets and dip into the batter. Deep fry for 5–7 minutes, according to the thickness of the fillets, or until golden brown. Drain on kitchen paper and serve with wedges of lemon.

Krokettes psariou

Fish croquettes

4 SERVINGS

2 oz. butter
2 oz. flour
½ pint hot milk
salt and pepper
1½ lb. cooked fish

2–3 hard-boiled eggs
4 oz. grated cheese
egg and crumbs for frying
oil for shallow frying
chopped parsley

Melt the butter over gentle heat, add the flour and cook for 2–3 minutes. Gradually add the hot milk, season well and simmer until the sauce is thick. Remove from the heat. Shred the fish and chop the eggs into very small pieces. Mix into the sauce together with the cheese and more seasoning. Cover pan and let the mixture get quite cold. Drop spoonfuls of the mixture on to a floured pastry board, roll into sausages or small balls, dip in egg and crumbs and shallow fry in smoking hot oil until golden brown. Drain on kitchen paper, sprinkle with chopped parsley and serve immediately.

Psari tou fournou

Baked fish (1)

4 SERVINGS

2 lb. fresh haddock
or cod
chopped parsley
2 tablespoons
breadcrumbs
3–4 cloves garlic
salt and pepper

2–3 tomatoes
½ pint olive oil
4 tablespoons dry white
wine
2 tablespoons tomato
purée
juice 1 lemon

Clean, wash and cut the fish into portions. Sprinkle with salt. Mix the chopped parsley with the breadcrumbs, crushed garlic and add salt and pepper to taste. Put a layer in a greased fireproof dish and lay the fish cutlets on top. Cover with the rest of the parsley mixture. Peel and slice the tomatoes and place on top. Blend the oil, wine, tomato purée and lemon juice and carefully pour over. Cook in a moderate oven for 30–40 minutes.

Psari tou fournou

Baked fish (2)

6 SERVINGS

3 lb. haddock or hake
salt and pepper
½ pint dry white wine
¼ pint water
3 teaspoons mustard

3 teaspoons cornflour
knob butter
3–4 sprigs chopped
  parsley

Clean and wash the fish but leave it whole. Place in a shallow baking dish, sprinkle with salt and pepper and add most of the wine, and water. Add the mustard, previously diluted in the rest of the wine. Cook in a moderate oven for 45 minutes, basting frequently with the liquid in the dish. Remove the fish to a serving dish and keep hot. Strain the stock into a small saucepan, dilute the cornflour with a little water and add to the stock. Adjust the seasoning and mix in the knob of butter. Bring to the boil once and pour over the fish. Sprinkle with the chopped parsley.

Psari feta me saltsa

Fish cutlets with sauce

4 SERVINGS

4 fish cutlets
oil for frying
1 small onion, chopped
little seasoned flour
4 tomatoes, skinned

1 clove garlic
salt and pepper
1 tablespoon chopped
 parsley
¼ pint white wine

Wash and dry the cutlets. Heat the oil in a frying pan
and fry the finely chopped onion until just beginning
to colour. Dip the fish cutlets in the seasoned flour and
fry with the onion for 2 minutes. Turn with a slice and
fry the other side for a further 2 minutes. Peel and chop
the tomatoes, crush the garlic with a little salt and add
to the frying pan with the parsley, thyme, salt and pepper,
and pour in the wine. Cover with a lid and cook over
very low heat for 15 minutes.

Psari gratini

Fish au gratin

4–6 SERVINGS

Sauce:

1 lb. cod or haddock,
 skinned and boned
1–2 onions
2–3 carrots
2 sticks celery
2 sprigs parsley
salt and pepper
mashed potatoes

1 oz. butter
2 tablespoons flour
¼ pint hot milk
¼ pint hot fish stock
salt and pepper
2 tablespoons capers

4 tablespoons grated
 cheese
knob of butter

Put the roughly chopped onions, carrots, celery and
parsley in a saucepan, add salt and pepper to taste and

cover with water. Boil for 15 minutes, lower the heat and add the prepared fish. Simmer until cooked. Remove from the stock and flake, using two forks. Press the onions and carrots only through a sieve and mix with the fish. In the meantime melt the butter in a small saucepan, add the flour and cook gently for 2–3 minutes. Add gradually the hot milk and fish stock, season to taste and let it simmer until sauce thickens. Remove from the heat and add the capers. Combine fish with caper sauce. In a greased fireproof dish put a layer of mashed potatoes, add the fish mixture and cover with the rest of the potatoes. Top with the grated cheese and brush with the melted knob of butter. Cook in a moderate oven for 20 minutes or until the top is golden brown.

Psari roullo

Fish loaf

4 SERVINGS

1½ lb. cooked fish
2 thick slices bread
¼ pint milk
3 eggs, separated
salt and pepper
1 tablespoon melted
  butter

1 tablespoon toasted
  breadcrumbs
1 teaspoon chopped
  parsley for decor-
  ation

Remove skin and bones and mash fish to a paste. Soak the bread in milk for 10–15 minutes and add to the fish. Stir in the egg yolks and season well. Mix thoroughly and fold in the stiffly beaten egg whites. Brush a loaf tin with melted butter and sprinkle with the bread-crumbs. Pack in the fish mixture and bake in a moderate oven for about 1 hour. Test with the blade of a knife: if it comes out clean, the loaf is cooked. Garnish with parsley. This dish can be eaten hot or cold.

Skoumbri tis scaras

Grilled mackerel

4 SERVINGS

4 medium-sized mackerel
salt
4 tablespoons olive oil
3–4 sprigs thyme

1–2 tablespoons lemon
juice
chopped parsley

Clean, wash and score the mackerel in 2–3 places on each side. Rub with salt inside and out and leave to drain. Brush the fish with a little of the oil and place under the grill, not too close to the heat. Tie the sprigs of thyme together. Mix the oil and lemon juice. Dip the bunch of thyme into the oil mixture and brush the mackerel occasionally until golden brown. Turn and repeat on the other side until the fish is cooked through. Remove on to a dish and pour the rest of the oil and lemon mixture on top. Sprinkle with the chopped parsley and serve immediately.

Skoumbri yahni

Ragoût of mackerel

4 SERVINGS

2 lb. fresh mackerel
salt and pepper
juice ½ lemon
8 tablespoons olive oil
2 large onions, chopped
¼ pint dry white wine
1 tablespoon chopped dill

2 tablespoons chopped
parsley
4 tablespoons tomato
purée
little water

Clean, wash and cut fish into serving portions. Sprinkle with salt and lemon juice and leave aside. Heat the olive oil and fry the finely chopped onions until golden brown. Add the wine, chopped dill and parsley, tomato purée previously diluted in a little water, and seasoning to taste. Cover the pan with a lid and simmer for 10–15 minutes. Dry the fish and lower into the sauce, which should cover it completely. Cook gently for 15–20 minutes, or until the fish is tender and the sauce rich and thick. This dish can be eaten hot or cold.

Bakaliaros freskos me rizi

Cod and rice casserole

6 Servings

2½ lb. cod cutlets
salt and pepper
½ lemon
⅛ pint olive oil
3 finely chopped onions
5 tomatoes
¼ pint white wine
1 clove garlic
1 tablespoon chopped parsley
4 oz. rice

Rub the fish cutlets with salt, pepper and lemon and place in a greased casserole. Heat the olive oil and fry the chopped onions until just beginning to colour. Add these to the casserole with the peeled crushed garlic, finely chopped tomatoes, parsley, seasoning and wine. Partly cook the rice in boiling salted water, drain and add to the other ingredients. Cover and bake in a moderate oven for 30 minutes, or a little longer according to the thickness of the cutlets.

Sardeles psites sto fourno

Fresh sardines baked in vine leaves

4–6 SERVINGS

2 lb. fresh sardines,
  sprats, smelts or small
  herring
salt and pepper

juice 1 lemon
vine leaves
olive oil

Clean the sardines and sprinkle with salt, pepper and lemon juice. Wrap a vine leaf round each fish and arrange on a shallow baking dish. Brush the vine leaves with a little oil and cook in a moderate oven for 20–25 minutes. Remove the leaves and serve immediately. The vine leaf and lemon juice impart a very subtle flavour to the fish, but only use fresh vine leaves, not the canned variety.

Sardeles tou fournou

Baked fresh sardines

4 SERVINGS

2 lb. fresh sardines
salt and pepper
1 large slice toast
1 egg
2 tablespoons grated
  cheese

4 tablespoons olive
  oil
toasted breadcrumbs
lemon slices

Clean the fish and remove the heads. Split open and remove the backbone. Salt lightly. Soak the slice of toast in tepid water and squeeze dry. Mix in the lightly beaten egg, salt, pepper and cheese. Spread some of this mixture on each sardine and fold back to its original shape. Place on a baking sheet, pour over the olive oil and sprinkle with breadcrumbs. Bake in a hot oven for about 30 minutes. Serve with lemon slices.

Soupies yahni

Cuttlefish in onion sauce

4–5 SERVINGS

1½–2 lb. cuttlefish
1 lb. sliced onions
scant ⅓ pint olive oil
½ pint dry white wine

½ bunch chopped parsley
salt and pepper
¼ pint water
(approximately)

Wash the fish in plenty of water and remove the head, entrails and inkbag. Remove the grey skin from the inkbag and cut the rest into thin strips, keeping a little of the ink. Cut the feelers from the head and chop them into 3–4 pieces. Heat the olive oil in a saucepan and fry the onion slices until golden brown. Add the fish, feelers and inkbag and fry for a few more minutes. Add the wine, hot water, parsley, salt and pepper. Cover the pan and cook slowly until the fish is very tender in a thick rich onion sauce. Cuttlefish requires long slow cooking.

Glosses tou fourno

Baked sole

4 SERVINGS

4 small soles
6 tablespoons dry white wine
3 tablespoons water
1 oz. butter
1 oz. flour

2 egg yolks
2 tablespoons toasted crumbs
1 oz. grated cheese
salt and pepper
knob butter

Clean and wash the fish, but leave whole. Arrange in a skillet and cover with the wine and water, and add a good pinch of salt. Simmer for 6–7 minutes, remove from the stock and drain on kitchen paper. Melt the butter, add the flour and cook for 2–3 minutes, stirring all the while. Add the stock gradually, adjust the seasoning and cook over low heat until the sauce thickens. Cool slightly and add the 2 egg yolks. Grease a shallow baking dish, sprinkle with 1 tablespoon breadcrumbs and arrange the fish on top. Spread the sauce over evenly and sprinkle with the rest of the crumbs and the grated cheese. Cut the knob of butter into tiny dice and dot all over the surface. Bake in a moderate oven until golden brown for 20–30 minutes.

Glosses me saltsa

Sole in sauce

4 SERVINGS

4 small sole
juice ½ lemon
seasoned flour
oil for frying

Sauce:

little oil
2–3 tablespoons flour
6 tablespoons white wine
2 tablespoons vinegar
2 tablespoons tomato
    purée
4 tablespoons water
salt and pepper
1 tablespoon chopped
    parsley
1–2 sprigs rosemary

Clean and wash the fish, sprinkle with lemon juice, dip in seasoned flour and fry quickly in hot olive oil. Drain and place on a hot dish and keep warm. Add a little more oil to the frying pan and mix in the flour. Cook, stirring constantly with a wooden spoon until the flour turns brown. Pour in the wine, vinegar, tomato purée diluted in the water, salt, pepper and flavouring herbs. Simmer gently for 15 minutes, stirring occasionally. Strain the sauce over the fish and serve hot.

Bakaliaros me saltsa

Salt cod with sauce

4 SERVINGS

1 lb. dried salt cod
water
olive oil for frying
seasoned flour

Sauce:

4 tablespoons olive oil
2 large onions
1 oz. flour
fish stock from cod
$\frac{1}{4}$ pint wine
3 tomatoes, chopped
  and skinned
4 cloves garlic
1 bay leaf
1 sprig rosemary
1 sprig marjoram
2 cloves
1 tablespoon walnuts
1 tablespoon capers
6 black stoned olives
salt and pepper

Cut the cod into small pieces and soak overnight in cold water to remove the salt. Next day put in fresh water and leave for a further 2–3 hours. Rinse well and remove skin and bones. Put these in a small saucepan, cover with $\frac{1}{2}$ pint water and simmer gently until liquid is reduced by half. Reserve this stock. Heat the oil in a frying pan, dip the cod pieces in seasoned flour and fry until golden brown. Keep in a warm place. Put the 4 tablespoons of olive oil in a skillet, add the finely chopped onion and fry lightly. Mix in the flour and cook, stirring continuously until it turns light brown. Strain the fish stock and add gradually. Pour in the wine, and when thoroughly blended add the tomatoes, crushed garlic, flavouring herbs and cloves. Boil steadily until the sauce is reduced by half. Strain, return to the pan and boil 2–3 times. Remove from the heat and add the finely chopped walnuts, capers and stoned olives. Season well, pour over the fish and serve at once.

Bakaliaros skordalia

Salt cod with garlic sauce

4–6 SERVINGS

2 lb. dry salt cod

Batter:

4 oz. sifted plain flour
$\frac{1}{4}$ teaspoon baking powder
$\frac{1}{4}$ pint tepid water
salt
olive oil for deep
   frying

Sauce:

4–5 cloves of garlic
1 teaspoon salt
4 oz. blanched almonds
1 medium-sized cooked
   potato
$\frac{1}{4}$ pint olive oil
$\frac{1}{8}$ pint wine vinegar
4–5 tablespoons water

Put the garlic with the salt in a mortar and pound to a smooth paste. Add the blanched almonds and continue pounding until all is well blended. Mash the potato and add to the other ingredients. Mix well and add the oil little by little. Pour in the vinegar and finally add the water. It should be the consistency of a thick mayonnaise.

Cut the cod into portions and soak in cold water — skin side upward — for 24 hours, changing the water at least twice. Rinse well and remove skin and any bones. Dry thoroughly, dip in the batter and fry in deep smoking hot oil until golden brown. Serve with sauce.

Note:

This sauce can be served with fried mussels, fried aubergines, potatoes, marrows, etc.

Barbounia tis skaras

Grilled red mullet

4 SERVINGS

4 red mullet	1 tablespoon lemon juice
salt	1 teaspoon chopped
flour	parsley
4 tablespoons olive oil	1 teaspoon chopped dill

Clean and wash the mullet, but do not remove the heads or tails. Sprinkle with salt inside and outside and leave for a few minutes. Heat the grill and grease the grid with olive oil. Lightly dust the fish with flour and brush with a little olive oil. Place on the grid, not too near the heat, and cook until golden brown. Turn once. Beat the olive oil with lemon juice and parsley and pour over the fish while hot. Sprinkle the dill on top.

Xifios souvlakia

Sword-fish on skewers

4 SERVINGS

1½ lb. sword-fish	little oil
4–6 small firm tomatoes	salt and pepper
8 small bay leaves	lemon wedges

Wash and cut the fish into 1-inch cubes and thread on to 4 long skewers, alternating with halved tomatoes and bay leaves. Brush with olive oil, salt and pepper and place under a grill, not too close to the heat. Cook gently until the fish is tender — about 10–12 minutes. Garnish with wedges of lemon.

Sword-fish has a firm meaty flesh and is really delicious. It is very popular with foreign visitors to Greece. Halibut could be cooked in the same way, if sword-fish is unobtainable.

Ktapodi stiffado

Ragoût of octopus

8 SERVINGS

1 2-lb. octopus
¼ pint olive oil
1 lb. pickling onions
½ pint red wine
3 cloves garlic

2 tablespoons tomato
 purée
1 bay leaf
salt and pepper

Soak the octopus for a few hours in cold water. Rinse well and cut the body and the tentacles into 1-inch cubes. Place in a saucepan without any liquid and toss over gentle heat until the pieces begin to turn red. Heat the olive oil in a saucepan and sauté the onions. Add the octopus, the wine, crushed garlic, tomato purée, bay leaf and seasoning, cover the pan and cook very gently for 3–4 hours or until the octopus is really tender.

Garides tiganites

Fried prawns

4 SERVINGS

12 oz. prepared prawns
1 egg, separated
4 tablespoons milk
3 oz. sifted flour
1 teaspoon baking
 powder

salt and pepper
1 dessertspoon olive
 oil
oil for frying
parsley

Beat the egg yolk with the oil and stir in the milk. Add the flour previously sifted with the baking powder and seasoning, and beat well to obtain a smooth batter. Fold in the stiffly beaten egg white. Dip the prawns in the batter and fry in smoking hot oil. Serve with fried parsley. Dip sprigs of parsley in ice-cold water and dry well and fry quickly in the oil. Serve immediately, otherwise it loses its crispness.

Garides me saltsa

Prawns in wine sauce

4 Servings

3 oz. butter or 6 table-
spoons olive oil
1 chopped onion
1 lb. ripe tomatoes
1 pint peeled prawns
$\frac{1}{4}$ pint dry, white wine

1 tablespoon chopped
parsley
salt and pepper
3–4 tablespoons water
1 tablespoon brandy
(optional)

Heat the butter or oil in a saucepan and fry the chopped
onion until golden brown. Peel and rub the tomatoes
through a sieve and add to the pan with the wine, chopped
parsley, seasoning and 3–4 tablespoons water. Cover the
pan and simmer until the sauce begins to thicken. Add
the prawns and cook slowly for a further 10 minutes.
If the sauce is made with butter this dish is eaten hot,
but if you would like to serve it cold you must prepare
it with olive oil. For an extra touch of luxury stir in
1 tablespoon brandy just before bringing the dish to
the table.

Soufflé garides

Prawn soufflé

4–6 Servings

3 tablespoons butter
4 tablespoons flour
$\frac{1}{4}$ pint hot milk
salt and pepper

3 eggs, separated
$\frac{1}{2}$ pint prepared prawns,
chopped

Heat the butter, add the flour mixed with the seasoning
and stir over gentle heat until well blended. Pour on the
hot milk gradually and cook until the sauce thickens.
Remove from the heat, season, and add the chopped

prawns. Add the beaten egg yolks and fold in the stiffly beaten egg whites very lightly. Pour the mixture in a well-buttered soufflé case and bake in a moderate oven for 30 minutes. Serve at once.

Midia gratin

Mussels au gratin

4 SERVINGS

2 quarts mussels
½ pint dry white wine
1½ oz. butter
2 tablespoons flour
salt and pepper
1 egg yolk

1 tablespoon chopped parsley
cream or top of milk
toasted breadcrumbs
1–2 oz. butter, cut into dice

Scrub the mussels to remove sand and grit and wash under running water. Put in a saucepan with the wine, cover with a lid and cook gently until the shells open. Remove the flesh, and put aside and strain the liquor into a bowl. Melt the butter in a small saucepan, add the flour and cook for 1–2 minutes, stirring all the while. Stir in the liquor from the mussels, season well and cook over low heat until the sauce thickens. Remove from the heat, beat in the egg yolk, add the chopped parsley and enough cream to make a thick sauce. Choose the largest of the shells and put 2–3 mussels in each one. Cover with the sauce and place on a baking tray close together. Sprinkle with the toasted crumbs and dot with the butter. Place in a moderate oven to brown the tops lightly. Serve hot or cold.

Meat Dishes

Say 'meat' to a Greek and ten to one the answer will be lamb. This would be followed by veal, pork, beef, but hardly ever mutton — it is not popular. However, the height of gastronomic experience is baby lamb, *arnaki galaktos* and sucking pig! Baby lamb at Easter and sucking pig on New Year's Eve: these are two of the most important festivals in the Greek calendar, when people really 'go to town' with food.

Christmas is essentially a religious and family affair, and though in more sophisticated circles there is a tendency now to adopt the Western way of celebrating, I doubt if this will spread.

Traditionally, the Easter lamb is roasted on a spit over a wood or charcoal fire in the open air, and on Easter Sunday one can small the delicious aroma hanging all over town and country alike. Though it is a far cry from lamb on the spit

I am giving you a recipe for lamb chunks grilled on skewers, *souvlakia*, which are very popular and really delicious, as well as being easy and simple to cook. Some of the Greek stuffings for meat are also rather unusual and very tasty.

The success of all Greek meat dishes depends upon the choice of tender cuts of meat. Cheaper cuts may be substituted for the sake of economy, but for perfect results use the cuts suggested in the recipe.

Frikasse me maroulia

Lamb fricassée with lettuce

6–8 Servings

4 oz. butter or margarine
3 lb. shoulder of lamb
salt and pepper
12 spring onions
$\frac{1}{4}$ pint water
3 lettuces

2 tablespoons chopped
  dill
2 egg yolks
2 lemons

Heat the butter in a large saucepan and add the meat cut into neat portions. Chop the spring onions, including most of the green part, and add to the meat. Season well and cover with $\frac{1}{4}$ pint of water. Simmer for 20–30 minutes. Trim, wash and cut the lettuce into pieces and add to the pan with the chopped dill and very little water. Cover the pan and cook over low heat until the meat is tender. In a small basin beat the egg yolks with 3–4 tablespoons lemon juice (more or less according to taste) and gradually add the stock from the pan, stirring continuously. Return this mixture to the saucepan and cook for 1–2 minutes for the sauce to thicken, but do not allow it to boil after the eggs have been added.

Arni stithos me kolokithakia

Breast of lamb with courgettes

6 Servings

3 lb. breast of lamb
4 oz. butter or margarine
8 tablespoons water
salt and pepper
6 spring onions

$\frac{1}{4}$ pint hot water
2 lb. courgettes
2 egg yolks
2 tablespoons lemon
  juice

Cut the meat into serving portions. Melt the butter, toss in the meat and add 8 tablespoons water. Bring to the boil, skim and add salt and pepper to taste and the spring onions cut in small pieces (white part only). Cover with $\frac{1}{4}$ pint hot water and simmer gently for 30 minutes. Scrape, wash and cut the courgettes into thick rounds. Add to the meat and cook slowly until both meat and courgettes are tender. Remove the meat and vegetables on to a dish and keep warm. Strain the stock and return to the pan. Beat the egg yolks with the lemon juice and gradually pour in the hot stock, stirring all the while. Empty this back into the saucepan and cook until the sauce thickens, without bringing it to the boil. Pour the sauce over the meat and courgettes.

Giouvetsi

Lamb with pasta

4–6 SERVINGS

2–3-lb. leg or shoulder of lamb	1 lb. tomatoes
salt and pepper	2 pints hot water
4 oz. butter	1 lb. pasta (noodles or cut macaroni)

Wipe the meat with a damp cloth and cut into serving portions — about the size of an egg. Sprinkle with salt and pepper and put into an earthenware dish (*giouvetsi*) with the butter. Cook in a hot oven until the meat begins to brown. Skin and cut the tomatoes in small pieces, place on top of the meat, lower the heat of the oven and continue to cook for 30 minutes. Add the hot water gradually, season well and add the pasta. Continue to cook until both meat and pasta are very tender. Bring the giouvetsi to the table and serve with a plain green salad.

Arnaki Yemisto

Stuffed lamb

6–8 SERVINGS

1 shoulder of lamb	salt and pepper
6 oz. butter	½ teaspoon mixed spice
1 medium-sized chopped onion	2–3 tablespoons brandy
12 oz. lambs' liver	1 tablespoon tomato purée
4 rounded tablespoons rice	2–3 tablespoons water
2–3 tablespoons pine kernels	2 tablespoons currants

Melt 4 oz. butter in a saucepan and toss in the onion. Mince or chop the liver very fine and add to the pan. Fry lightly for 5–6 minutes and stir in the rice, pine kernels, salt, pepper and spice. Mix thoroughly and pour in the brandy and the tomato purée, previously diluted in the water. Simmer gently until all the liquid is absorbed. Remove from the heat and stir in the currants. Bone the shoulder and wipe with a damp cloth. Make a deep pocket and sprinkle with salt and pepper. Stuff with the liver mixture and close the opening by rough sewing. Rub all over with the cut lemon and sprinkle with salt and pepper. Place on a trivet in a roasting tin, put the remaining butter on top and roast in a moderate oven for 1–1½ hours depending on size.

Arnaki sto harti

Lamb cooked in paper **(1)**

6–8 SERVINGS

1 3-lb. leg of lamb	salt and pepper
1 clove garlic	2 oz. feta or gruyère cheese
1 lemon	butter
1 teaspoon marjoram or thyme	

Wipe the meat with a damp cloth, and insert the clove of garlic deeply into the knuckle end. Rub the meat with lemon juice and the marjoram or thyme, and sprinkle with salt and pepper to taste. Have ready well buttered greaseproof paper and lay the meat on it. Cut the cheese into thin slices and put on top of the meat. Wrap grease-proof paper round it to make a neat parcel and tie with string. Place on a baking tray and cook in a moderate oven for 2 hours, with the cheese side always on top. Bring to the table in the paper case and serve very hot.

Arnaki sto harti

Lamb cooked in paper (2)

6–8 SERVINGS

1 3-lb. leg of lamb	2 hard-boiled eggs
3–4 tablespoons olive oil	2 cloves garlic
1 tablespoon lemon juice	salt and pepper
1 tablespoon chopped parsley	4 oz. cheese
1 teaspoon marjoram or thyme	

Wipe the meat with a damp cloth and cut into 8 portions. Put oil, lemon juice, parsley, thyme, chopped eggs and garlic and the meat in a basin. Season well and mix thoroughly. Cut greaseproof paper slightly larger than the meat pieces, place a portion of meat and egg on each paper, cover with a slice of cheese and fold over the paper. Crinkle the edges over like a Cornish pasty to make a tight little case, and place on a baking sheet as close together as possible. Cook in a moderate oven for 1–1½ hours.

Kreatopitta Kefalonias

Meat pie (Cephalonia style)

6 SERVINGS

Filling:

1 1½-lb. leg of lamb (lean)
1 large potato
3 tablespoons rice
grated orange rind
1 chopped onion
2 cloves garlic
4 tomatoes, chopped
  and peeled
salt and pepper
3 oz. grated cheese
1 tablespoon chopped
  parsley
1 teaspoon chopped mint
1 oz. melted butter
1 tablespoon olive oil
¼ pint stock, wine or water
2-3 hard-boiled eggs

Pastry:

12 oz. flour
5-6 tablespoon olive oil
water to mix
salt

Glaze:

little melted butter

Cut the meat and potato into cubes and put in a bowl. Add the rice, rind, chopped onion, garlic, tomatoes, grated cheese, parsley, mint and seasoning, and mix in the butter and oil. Gradually add about ¼ pint liquid and mix thoroughly.

Sift the flour with the salt into a mixing bowl, add the olive oil and mix with a fork, gradually adding enough cold water to make a stiff dough. Turn on to a well-floured board and divide into two portions. Roll one portion into a circle ¼ inch thick and slightly larger than your pie plate, and carefully lift it into the greased plate. Add the filling and arrange the slices of hard-boiled eggs on top. Roll the remaining pastry into a circle ⅛ inch thick and about 2 inches wider than the plate, moisten the edge and press firmly on to the bottom crust.

Turn the overhanging pastry under to prevent the juices from oozing, and press firmly. Crimp the edges and brush the top with a little melted butter. Bake in a moderate oven for about 1 hour or until the pastry is golden brown.

Arni me fassolakia freska

Shoulder of lamb with green beans

4–6 Servings

2 lb. French or runner beans
1 2½-lb. shoulder of lamb
4–6 oz. butter
3 chopped onions
1 lb. ripe tomatoes
salt and pepper
2 tablespoons chopped parsley

Trim and slice the beans, but not too thinly, and place in a bowl of water. Cut the meat into portions. Heat the butter in a saucepan and brown the meat and onions. Rub the tomatoes through a sieve, or peel and chop very small, and add to the pan. Season and cover with a lid. Cook gently for 15 minutes. Drain the beans and add to the meat with the chopped parsley, seasoning and very little water. Put a saucer on top to keep the beans well immersed in the liquid, cover the pan with a lid and simmer until both meat and beans are tender.

Souvlakia

Lamb grilled on skewers

6 SERVINGS

1 2-lb. leg of lamb (fillet)	½ teaspoon marjoram or thyme
2 small onions	salt and pepper
2–3 tablespoons olive oil	12 bay leaves
juice ½ lemon	6 small tomatoes

Trim and cut the meat into 1-inch cubes. From the fat end of the joint cut some very small pieces of fat and put them all together in a basin. Peel and quarter the onions, separate the pieces and add to the contents of the basin. Pour in the olive oil and sprinkle with lemon juice, marjoram and a good pinch of pepper. Mix well and leave for 30–40 minutes or even overnight, to allow the meat to get well impregnated with the oil and the flavourings. Thread the meat on to six 9–10-inch skewers interspersed here and there with a piece of fat, onion, bay leaf and half tomato, until the skewer is full. Grill for 15 minutes, not too close to the heat, turning them from time to time for even cooking. When ready, sprinkle with salt and serve on the skewers, with a plain salad or on a bed of rice.

Arni fournou me melidzanes

Roast lamb with aubergines

4–5 SERVINGS

1 2-lb. leg of lamb	4 oz. melted butter
salt and pepper	4 medium-sized
4 large ripe tomatoes	aubergines

Wipe the meat with a damp cloth and sprinkle with salt and pepper. Peel and slice the tomatoes and arrange in a roasting tin. Season well. Place the meat on top of the tomato slices, pour over the melted butter and cook in a moderate oven for 25-30 minutes. In the meantime, cut the aubergines into thick rounds and drop in salted cold water for 15 minutes. Rinse and dry well. Arrange the aubergines round the meat, dust with a little salt and pepper and continue cooking for about 30 minutes until both the meat and vegetables are tender.

Arnaki me antidia

Lamb with chicory

4–5 SERVINGS

3 oz. butter
4–5 lean lamb chops
1 large chopped
   onion
2 tablespoons water

1 rounded tablespoon
   flour
salt and pepper
4 heads chicory
1 bottle yoghurt

Heat the butter in a saucepan and lightly sauté the chops and onion without letting them colour. Add the water and stir in the flour. Season to taste and mix until all the ingredients are well blended. Cover with water. In the meantime remove the outer coarse leaves of the chicory and cut into thick slices. Drop these into the pan, cover and simmer gently until the meat and chicory are tender and there is very little liquid left in the pan. Stir in the yoghurt gradually and bring to the boil 2–3 times. The sauce should be thick and creamy.

Arnaki tou fournou

Roast spring lamb

6 SERVINGS

1 shoulder or leg of
   lamb
salt and pepper
juice 1 lemon
1 clove garlic
   (optional)

1 lb. potatoes
1 lb. tomatoes
1 teaspoon chopped
   parsley
½ teaspoon chopped mint
2–3 oz. melted butter

Wipe the meat with a damp cloth and rub well with salt, pepper and lemon juice. Make a slit near the knuckle and push in the garlic, if used. Arrange the meat and potatoes in a roasting tin. Cut the tomatoes in half and place on top of the meat, season them and sprinkle over the parsley and mint. Pour in the melted butter and cook in a moderate oven for about 1 hour or until the meat is tender.

Arni me damaskina ke amygdala

Lamb stew with prunes and almonds

6 SERVINGS

1 2½-lb. shoulder or leg
   of lamb
1 onion
salt and pepper
juice 1 lemon
2 oz. butter

1 tablespoon flour
stock or water
1 lb. prunes (soaked)
8 oz. shelled almonds
2 tablespoons sugar

Cut the meat into small pieces and put into a bowl with the sliced onion, seasoning and lemon juice. Leave for at least one hour. Heat the butter in a saucepan, drain the meat and brown lightly. Stir in the flour and fry until brown. Pour in enough stock or water to barely cover the meat, put a lid on the pan and simmer for 40–45 minutes. Add the prunes and almonds and cook until tender. Lastly mix in the sugar and a little lemon juice and bring to the boil once before serving.

Note:

Best stewing lamb may be used in this recipe, but the result will not have the same delicious flavour.

Arni me kastana

Lamb stew with chestnuts

4–6 SERVINGS

2 lb. chestnuts	1 tablespoon flour
2 lb. lamb	½ pint meat stock
1 onion	salt and pepper
2 oz. butter	1 level tablespoon sugar

Score the chestnuts and bake in the oven until shell and inside skin will peel off easily. Cut the meat into small pieces and slice the onions. Heat the butter in a stew pan and sauté the meat and onions. Sprinkle in the flour and cook until well browned. Mix in about ½ pint meat stock, salt and pepper to taste and cover the pan with a lid. Simmer for 30 minutes and add the chestnuts. Cook for a further 50–60 minutes, or until the meat and chestnuts are very tender. Stir in the sugar just before the meal is ready.

Arni giouvetsi

Lamb casserole

4–6 SERVINGS

1 lb. aubergines	2 lb. lamb
salt and pepper	5 sliced tomatoes
1 lb. potatoes	$\frac{1}{2}$ pint hot water
3 medium-sized onions	3 oz. rice
3 medium-sized green	4 oz. melted butter
peppers	4 oz. grated cheese

Wipe the aubergines, cut into cubes and sprinkle with salt. Place on a dish and leave for 30 minutes. Rinse and dry. Peel and slice the potatoes and onions. De-seed and cut the peppers into rings. Cut the meat into thick slices. Put a layer of potatoes in an earthenware casserole (*giouvetsi*) and place the meat slices on top. Continue adding the different ingredients in layers and sprinkling each layer with salt, pepper and rice. Finish with a layer of sliced tomatoes. Carefully pour in the hot water and the melted butter. Cover the casserole with a lid and cook in a very moderate oven for 2 hours. Remove the lid and cover the top thickly with the grated cheese. Return to the oven and bake without a lid until the cheese turns golden brown.

Kotolettes sto harti

Chops cooked in paper

6 SERVINGS

6 lamb chops	3–4 tablespoons dry
seasoned flour	white wine
2–3 oz. butter	salt and pepper
2–3 medium-sized onions	1 tablespoon parsley
2 cloves garlic	2 oz. ham
3 tomatoes	melted butter

Trim chops, dip them in seasoned flour and fry in butter for 12–15 minutes, according to size. Remove them to a dish. Chop the onions and garlic very fine and fry them until golden brown, add the peeled and sliced tomatoes, the chopped parsley, the wine and seasoning, and let the mixture simmer until reduced to a thick pulp. Remove from the heat and when cool add the ham cut up in small pieces. In the meantime, take 6 sheets of greaseproof paper, cut them slightly larger than the chops and shape them like a kidney (see diagram below). Fold the paper in two, grease it with melted butter and spread some of the tomato mixture on one half. Lay the chop on it and spread some more of the mixture on the chop. Fold the other half of the paper over and twist the edges all round to enclose the chop completely and form a small parcel. Place the parcels on a greased tray and bake in a moderate oven for about 15–20 minutes.

Note:

Instead of ham you can use smoked tongue, truffles, mushrooms or a mixture of any two of the above ingredients in the sauce.

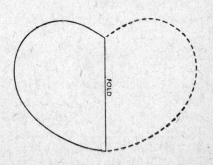

Kefalaki arnissio riganato

Roast lambs' heads with marjoram

4 SERVINGS

2 lambs' heads
lemon
salt and pepper
2 slices bread
2–3 tablespoons olive
  oil

1 tablespoon chopped
  parsley
1 teaspoon marjoram
1 tablespoon tomato
  purée or a few fresh
  tomatoes
little water

Split the heads in two, or better still get your butcher to
do it for you. Soak them in cold water until there is no
trace of blood showing. Rinse and rub them well with
a cut lemon, salt and pepper. Put them in a roasting tin,
cut side uppermost. To save the brains from getting
tough and discoloured place a thin slice of bread on each
side. In a little basin mix the oil, chopped parsley,
marjoram, salt and pepper, and tomato purée diluted
in a little water (or if fresh tomatoes are used, skinned
and chopped in very small pieces). Mix well and pour
over the heads in the tin. Roast in a moderate oven for
30–35 minutes, or until the meat is tender, basting
frequently with the liquid in the tin.

Note:

The heads for this dish must come from very young
animals.

You can buy real Greek marjoram (*rigani*) from Greek
or Cypriot shops.

Arni me koukia avgolemono

Lamb with broad beans and egg and lemon sauce

6 SERVINGS

2-lb. shoulder of lamb
1 oz. butter
4 tablespoons olive oil
1 chopped onion
1 tablespoon lemon juice
salt and pepper
½ pint hot water

4–5 spring onions
2 tablespoons chopped
 dill
2 lb. shelled broad beans
Avgolemono sauce
 (see page 194)

Wipe the meat and cut into serving pieces. Melt the butter, add the olive oil and fry the meat and chopped onion until brown. Add the lemon juice, salt and pepper and pour in hot water to cover. Put the lid on to the pan, lower the heat and simmer gently until the meat is almost cooked. Remove the meat on to a dish. Chop up the spring onions including the green part and add to the pan, also the dill and the broad beans. Cook gently for 15 minutes. Return the meat to the pan, adjust the seasoning, and if necessary add a little more hot water. Cover and cook gently for a further 30 minutes, or until both meat and beans are quite tender. Remove from the heat and add the Avgolemono sauce.

Note:

When the beans are very young and tender they can be cooked in their shells. Just string and slice them like runner beans. The flavour is delicious and you will need only 1 lb. of beans to the above ingredients.

Podarakia arniou avgolemono

Lambs' trotters in egg and lemon sauce

4–8 SERVINGS

8 lambs' trotters	2 oz. butter
1 onion	3 tablespoons flour
2 carrots	½ pint stock
2–3 stalks celery	2 egg yolks
2–3 sprigs parsley	1 lemon
salt and pepper	chopped parsley
water	

Split the trotters in two without separating them. Rinse well and put in a saucepan with the onion, carrot, celery and parsley, and season to taste. Add water to cover and cook slowly until the meat is tender and there is about ½ pint liquid left in the pan. Remove the trotters on to a dish and keep warm. Strain the stock and return to the pan. Melt the butter in a small saucepan and stir in the flour. Cook over gentle heat for 2–3 minutes and gradually pour in the hot stock, stirring constantly. Simmer until the sauce thickens and adjust the seasoning. Lightly beat the egg yolks with the lemon juice and mix into the sauce. Do not boil again. Pour the sauce over the trotters and sprinkle with the chopped parsley.

Note:

You can use tripe, instead of trotters, in this recipe, or tripe and trotters mixed.

Kapamas moraitikos

Lamb à la Morea

6–8 Servings

3 lb. leg of lamb	1 tablespoon tomato
seasoned flour	purée
2 oz. butter	salt and pepper
2 tablespoons flour	2–3 cloves
¼ pint dry white wine	pinch cinnamon
little water	

Cut the meat into fairly large pieces, about the size of an egg. Dip in seasoned flour and fry in the butter until well browned. Remove the meat. Add the flour to the butter in the frying pan, stir well with a wooden spoon until it turns dark brown, add the wine and a little water and let it simmer for a few minutes. Strain into a saucepan, add the pieces of meat, the tomato purée, previously diluted in a little water, the seasoning, the cloves and cinnamon. Cover well and let it simmer very gently until well cooked, about 45 minutes.

Kolokithia papoutsakia

Little shoes

4–6 Servings

2 lb. medium-sized
   courgettes
1 lb. minced veal or
   lamb
1 finely chopped onion
2½ oz. butter
¼ pint white wine
1 lb. fresh or canned
   tomatoes

1 tablespoon chopped
   parsley
½ teaspoon sugar
pinch cinnamon
salt and pepper
4 tablespoons grated
   cheese
2 eggs
2 tablespoons toasted
   breadcrumbs

Remove the stem end and wash the courgettes. Cut them
in halves lengthwise and plunge them in boiling salted
water. Cook for 5–6 minutes. Strain well and when cool
enough to handle scoop out the pulp carefully. Arrange
the shells close together in a baking dish. In the meantime,
put the minced meat and onion in a frying pan, add
a good pinch of pepper and cook for a few minutes.
When the meat looks dry add 1½ oz. of the butter and
fry until both meat and onion are nicely brown. Pour
in the wine and add the skinned and finely chopped
tomatoes, the parsley, sugar, cinnamon and salt. Cover
the pan with a lid and simmer gently until the mince
is cooked and all the liquid absorbed. Remove from the
heat, cool slightly and add half the cheese. Fill the
courgettes with this stuffing. Beat the eggs with the rest
of the cheese and pour over the courgettes. Sprinkle
with the toasted breadcrumbs. Melt the remaining butter
and carefully pour all over the dish. Bake in a moderate
oven for 30 minutes. Serve hot.

Youvarlakia me domata

Meat balls in tomato sauce

4–6 SERVINGS

1 lb. fresh, finely minced
  lamb or veal
1 tablespoon rice
1 egg
salt and pepper
little chopped mint
1 medium-sized onion

little water
1 bunch parsley
2–3 oz. butter
about $\frac{1}{4}$ pint hot water
1 tablespoon tomato
  purée

Put the minced meat in a basin and add the rice, beaten
egg, seasoning and chopped mint. Grate the onion and
parboil in a little salted water, just enough to soften.
Add to the mixture in the basin and knead until thoroughly blended. Chop the parsley very fine and spread
on a shallow dish. Take a spoonful of the mince and
drop it on to the parsley. Moisten your hands with cold
water and shape the mixture into a ball completely
covered with parsley. Continue until all the mixture is
used up. Melt the butter in a skillet. Lower the balls
carefully and do not put in more than two layers so as
not to spoil their shape. Pour some hot water, enough
to cover, in which you have diluted the tomato purée.
Simmer gently until cooked and the liquid is reduced
to a thick sauce. Serve hot.

Kefalaki moscari salata

Calf's head salad

6 Servings

1 calf's head
1 onion
2 carrots
2 sticks celery
3 sprigs parsley
1 bay leaf
water

salt and pepper
2–3 spring onions,
  finely chopped
1 teaspoon chopped
  parsley
6 tablespoons olive oil
pinch mustard

Soak the head in cold salted water for 2–3 hours. Rinse thoroughly and put in a large saucepan with the onion, carrots, celery, parsley and bay leaf. Pour in water to cover and season to taste. Bring to the boil, skim well and lower the heat. Simmer for 3–4 hours. Remove all the meat from the bones, skin and chop the tongue into small pieces. Strain the stock and add a few tablespoons to the meat. Pack into an oblong tin, put a weight on top and leave it to set. When ready, cut into thin slices and sprinkle with the spring onions and the teaspoon of chopped parsley. Mix the oil, mustard and vinegar, and when thoroughly blended pour over the meat slices.

Moscaraki roullo

Rolled veal pot-roast

4–6 Servings

1½ lb. fillet of veal
  cut in 1 piece
salt and pepper
2 tablespoons finely
  chopped parsley
2 cloves garlic
3 thin slices ham

3–4 thin slices cheese
3 oz. butter
4 tablespoons dry white
  wine
2 teaspoons tomato
  purée
¼ pint hot water

Beat fillet with a wooden mallet or a rolling pin until very thin. Sprinkle with salt, pepper, parsley and the finely chopped garlic. Arrange the slices of ham and place the cheese on top. Roll up and tie neatly with string. Heat the butter in a saucepan and lower in the meat roll. Brown all over and add the wine and the tomato purée diluted in the hot water. Adjust the seasoning and cook over gentle heat until the meat is tender.

Kotolettes moscarissies pane

Veal cutlets

1 egg
1 tablespoon water
salt and pepper
4 veal cutlets
2 tablespoons grated
  cheese

2–3 tablespoons toasted
  breadcrumbs
butter for frying
lemon wedges

Lightly beat the egg with the water. Season the cutlets well and cover with the grated cheese, dip in egg and roll in the breadcrumbs. Leave for 5 minutes. Fry the cutlets in the butter until golden brown on both sides. Serve with lemon wedges.

Escalopes me elies

Escalopes with black olives

4 SERVINGS

1½ lb. veal escalopes
(4–5 fillets)
2 oz. butter
4 tablespoons olive oil
seasoned flour
4 tablespoons wine
1 tablespoon lemon juice

1 clove garlic
1 sliced lemon
1 bay leaf
2 cloves
salt and pepper
4 oz. black olives
lemon slices

Cut the fillet into portions and pound well to flatten. Heat the butter and oil, dip the meat in the seasoned flour and fry until golden brown, turning once. Add the wine, lemon juice and all the other ingredients except the olives and lemon slices. Cover the pan and cook very gently for 40–45 minutes, or until tender. Add the stoned olives to the pan and cook for a further 2–3 minutes. Place the escalopes on a hot dish and surround with the olives and lemon slices. Strain the liquid into a sauce boat and serve separately.

Stithos moscari yemisto

Stuffed breast of veal

6 SERVINGS

1½ oz. butter
2 tablespoons olive oil
1 chopped onion
8 oz. minced veal or pork
3 tablespoons scalded
rice
1 large tomato
1 egg

1 tablespoon chopped
parsley
20 pistachio nuts
salt and pepper
1 breast of veal (2–2½ lb.)
1 tablespoon lemon juice
¼ pint wine
¼ pint water

Heat $\frac{1}{3}$ of the butter and 1 tablespoon oil and lightly fry the onion and the minced meat. Remove from the heat and add the rice, skinned and chopped tomato, lightly beaten egg, parsley, nuts and seasoning. Wipe the breast of veal with a damp cloth and cut in two lengthwise. Lay the stuffing on one piece and cover with the other. Close by roughly sewing all round. Heat the rest of the butter and oil in a skillet and lower in the meat. Brown well all over and pour in the wine, lemon juice and $\frac{1}{4}$ pint water. Cover and cook gently for 1–1$\frac{1}{2}$ hours.

Videlo me tyri

Veal stuffed with cheese

8 SERVINGS

1 3$\frac{1}{2}$-lb. shoulder of veal	5 cloves garlic
1$\frac{1}{2}$ oz. butter	juice 1 lemon
salt and pepper	$\frac{1}{4}$ pint white wine
8 oz. grated Parmesan cheese	

Bone the shoulder and cut open to form one long strip. Wipe with a damp cloth. Soften $\frac{1}{2}$ oz of the butter and spread it all over the surface of the meat. Season well with salt and pepper and cover with the grated cheese and finely chopped garlic. Roll up like a Swiss roll and tie securely with string. Melt the rest of the butter in a large saucepan and when quite hot lower in the meat carefully. Fry until nicely brown and add the lemon juice. Cover the saucepan, lower the heat and cook gently, adding a little wine now and then, until all is used up and the meat is quite tender. Remove the string and cut in slices.

Moscari me araka

Veal ragoût with peas

6 SERVINGS

1½ lb. stewing veal
3 oz. butter
2 finely chopped
  onions
1 lb. tomatoes

pinch sugar
salt and pepper
water
1 tablespoon chopped
  dill or parsley

Cut the meat into serving portions and brown in the hot butter with the finely chopped onions. Add the peeled and finely chopped tomatoes, the sugar, seasoning and enough water to cover the meat. Cover the saucepan with a lid and simmer for about 20 minutes. Add the shelled peas and the dill or parsley. Cover and cook until both meat and peas are tender and the sauce is thick and rich.

Youvarlakia me yaourti

Meat-balls with yoghurt (Cyprus style)

6–8 SERVINGS

1 large chopped onion
boiling water
1½ lb. minced veal
2 large slices toasted
  bread, minced
2 sprigs fresh mint
  (or dried)

3 tablespoons chopped
  parsley
salt and pepper
2 eggs
little flour
1¼ pints meat stock
1 lb. yoghurt (4 cartons)

Pour some boiling water on the finely chopped onion and leave for a few minutes. Drain well and mix with the meat, the ground toast, chopped mint and parsley, seasoning and lightly beaten eggs. When all the ingredients are thoroughly blended add a few drops of water as this makes the mixture lighter. Flour your hands and form into nut-sized balls. Bring the meat stock to the boil and stir in the rice. After 5 minutes fast boiling drop in the meat balls, lower the heat and cook covered until the rice and meat balls are tender. Remove the pan from the heat and take 4–5 tablespoons of the stock. Put the yoghurt into a bowl and beat well with a fork, gradually adding the meat stock. Pour the mixture over the contents of the pan and return to the heat to warm through but do not boil. Sprinkle a little more chopped mint on top and serve in hot soup bowls.

Escalopes yemistes

Stuffed escalopes

4 SERVINGS

4 large escalopes veal	4 hard-boiled eggs
3 oz. melted butter	2 tablespoons brandy
salt and pepper	2–3 tablespoons hot water

Pound the escalopes to flatten very thin. Spread with a little melted butter and sprinkle with salt and pepper. Place one hard-boiled egg on each escalope and roll up tightly. Secure with string. Heat the rest of the butter and lightly brown the meat. Pour in the brandy and hot water, adjust the seasoning and cover the pan with a lid. Cook on low heat for 15 minutes. Remove the string and serve.

Kydonato

Beef stew with quinces

6 SERVINGS

4 oz. butter
1 chopped onion
1½ lb. chuck steak

½ pint hot water
salt and pepper
1½ lb. quinces
2 teaspoons sugar

Melt the butter and fry the onions. Cut the meat into small pieces, add to the pan and brown all over. Pour in the water and add seasoning to taste. Peel the quinces, remove the core and cut into thick slices. Add these to the meat, sprinkle with the sugar and cover the pan with a lid. Cook slowly until the meat and the quinces are tender. The quantity of sugar can be varied to taste, but the characteristic of this dish is its sweetness.

Keftedes tis skaras

Grilled meat balls

6 SERVINGS

1½ lb. very finely minced
 steak
2–3 tablespoons finely
 chopped onion

1 tablespoon chopped
 parsley
salt and pepper
little oil or melted butter

Mix the steak, onion, parsley and seasoning. Dip your hands in cold water and shape the meat into medium-sized flat cakes. Brush with oil or melted butter and place on a greased grid under a hot grill. Cook for 3 minutes on each side.

Keftedes tiganiti

Fried meat balls

4 SERVINGS

12 oz. minced chuck steak
1 large chopped onion
2 tablespoons chopped
    parsley
salt and pepper

4 oz. breadcrumbs
1 egg
flour
fat for frying

Put the steak through the mincer twice and mix with the finely chopped onion, parsley and seasoning. Soak the breadcrumbs in water, squeeze dry and add to the meat. Bind with the beaten egg. Take one tablespoon of the mixture and form into a ball. Dip in flour to cover completely and deep fry until brown. These keftedes can be eaten cold, but in that case they must be fried in oil, not any other kind of fat, and if made very small they can be served on cocktail sticks.

Vodino stiffado

Ragoût of beef

4–6 SERVINGS

2 lb. chuck steak
¼ pint olive oil
1 finely chopped onion
¼ pint dry red wine
⅛ pint vinegar
1 lb. ripe tomatoes
2 cloves
1 small stick cinnamon

salt and pepper
1 bay leaf
2 lb. pickling onions
3 cloves garlic
4 oz. kefalotyri,
  or Parmesan
1 sprig rosemary

Cut the meat into portions. Heat half the olive oil and lightly brown the meat and finely chopped onion. Pour in the wine and vinegar, keeping 1 tablespoon vinegar for later use. Add the peeled and finely chopped tomatoes, spices, salt, pepper and bay leaf. Cover the pan with a lid and cook slowly. While the meat is simmering heat the rest of the oil in a small saucepan, add the pickling onions and garlic and cook covered until tender. Remove these with a perforated spoon and put into an earthenware casserole. Arrange the meat portions on top of the onions, rub the sauce through a sieve and add it to the casserole. Slice the cheese and fry quickly in the oil in which you fried the onions. Arrange the slices on top of the meat, sprinkle with the spoonful of vinegar and the sprig of rosemary and cook covered in a moderate oven for 40–45 minutes.

Skordostoumbi

Beef slices with garlic

4–5 Servings

1½ lb. chuck steak	2 tablespoons chopped
seasoned flour	parsley
oil for frying	salt and pepper
1 lb. peeled, sliced	2 tablespoons vinegar
tomatoes	6 tablespoons dry white
5 cloves garlic	wine

Cut the meat into small thin slices, dip in seasoned flour and fry in hot oil until nicely brown. Place the meat in a casserole, cover with the tomatoes and sprinkle with the finely chopped garlic, parsley and seasoning. Pour over any oil left over from frying, the vinegar and wine and enough hot water to cover. Put a lid on and cook slowly until the meat is tender in a thick rich sauce.

Gourounopoulo sto fourno

Roast pork

6 Servings

1 2½-lb. leg of pork	flour
1 lemon	2 lb. potatoes
salt and pepper	3 oz. olive oil

Wipe the meat and rub well with the ½ lemon and salt and pepper. Sprinkle with flour and place in a roasting tin. Peel medium-sized potatoes, sprinkle with salt and pepper and arrange in the tin. Carefully spoon the olive oil and juice of ½ lemon over the pork and cook in a moderately hot oven for 1½ hours, or until tender. The oil and lemon juice give the pork an unusual and very pleasant flavour. In Greece, they cook a whole sucking pig in this way.

Patsas tou fournou

Baked tripe

4 SERVINGS

2 lb. tripe
1½ lemons
1 small onion
1–2 carrots
1 stick celery
2 sprigs parsley
salt and peppercorns

boiling water
3 tablespoons olive oil
3 tablespoons toasted
 breadcrumbs
1 teaspoon chopped
 parsley

Wash the tripe and rub well with the ½ lemon. Put in a saucepan with the onion, carrots, celery and parsley sprigs and season to taste with salt and peppercorns. Add enough boiling water to cover and simmer gently for about 3 hours. Remove from the pan, dry thoroughly and cut into small pieces. Mix in a basin the oil with the juice of 1 lemon and parsley and add the tripe. Stir well and leave for 30–40 minutes, turning the pieces occasionally in the liquid. Remove the pieces of tripe carefully and roll them in the toasted breadcrumbs. Put them in a greased fireproof dish and bake in a moderate oven until golden brown.

Hirino me fassolia

Pork with butter beans

6 SERVINGS

1½ lb. butter beans
3–4 oz. butter
3 lb. lean pork
1 large chopped
  onion
1 tablespoon tomato
  purée

2 tablespoons chopped
  parsley
salt and pepper
¾ pint hot water

Soak the beans for 12 hours. Heat the butter in a sauce-pan and brown the meat, cut into small pieces. Add the onion and fry until golden brown. Dilute the tomato purée in ¼ pint hot water and add to the pan with the parsley and seasoning. Add ½ pint hot water and continue to cook over low heat. In the meantime drain the beans and put them to boil with enough water to cover. After 15 minutes, drain the beans and add them to the meat. Cook for a further 40–45 minutes, or until meat and beans are very tender.

Aphelia

Pork steeped in wine and coriander

4 SERVINGS

1½ lb. tenderloin or leg
  of pork
1 tablespoon ground
  coriander

dry red or white wine
salt and pepper

Cut the meat into small pieces, put in a basin and sprinkle with salt, pepper and coriander. Mix well and pour in enough wine to cover. Leave for 24 hours or longer. Transfer to an earthenware casserole with a tightly fitting lid and cook in a slow oven for 2–2½ hours.

Hirines brizoles tiganites

Fried pork chops

4 SERVINGS

4 pork chops	½ oz. butter
salt and pepper	2–3 teaspoons lemon
2 tablespoons water	juice

Sprinkle the chops with salt and pepper and put in the frying pan with the water. Bring to the boil and skim well. When there is no water left and the chops begin to sizzle, add the butter and fry until the chops are golden brown on both sides. Add the lemon juice and cook for a further 2 minutes.

Hirines brizoles tou fournou

Baked pork chops

4 SERVINGS

4 pork chops	1 stick celery
salt and pepper	1 ½ oz. melted butter
flour	2 teaspoons tomato purée
fat for frying	¼ pint hot water
2 medium-sized onions	4 tablespoons dry wine
2 large carrots	
2 potatoes	

Wipe the chops, sprinkle with salt and pepper, dip in flour and fry until golden brown. Cut the onions, carrots and potatoes into rounds and finely chop the celery. Put half the vegetables in a baking dish, sprinkle with salt and pepper and pour the butter on top. Add the chops and cover with the rest of the vegetables. Dilute the tomato purée in the hot water, pour in the dish and bake in a hot oven for 15 minutes. Add the wine, lower the heat and cook for a further 15–20 minutes.

Hirino kefali pikti

Pig's head mould

6 SERVINGS

1 pig's head
(including tongue)
1¼ pints dry white wine
¼ pint vinegar
2 onions
½ pint water
2 carrots
1 stick celery
salt and pepper
4 cloves
3 bay leaves
2–3 sprigs parsley
2 sprigs thyme
pinch mixed spice

Put the head to soak in salted water. Rinse and return to the pan with fresh water to cover and boil for 5 minutes. Throw away this water, rinse and return the head to the pan. Pour in the wine, the vinegar and ½ pint water and add the flavouring vegetables, the spice and a good pinch of salt, and pepper. Bring gradually to the boil and cook gently for 3 hours. Remove the head from the pan, pick all the meat and cut into very small dice. Skin the tongue and cut into small pieces. Mix with the meat, adjust the seasoning and pack into a mould or pudding basin. Strain the stock and pour on to the meat. Cover with a plate and leave for 12 hours to set.

Hirino avgolemono

Pork with egg and lemon sauce

6 SERVINGS

1 2-lb. leg of pork
2 chopped onions
½ pint water
salt and pepper
1 bay leaf

1 lb. sliced potatoes
2 egg yolks
2 tablespoons lemon
  juice
2 sprigs parsley

Wipe the meat with a damp cloth and cut into small pieces. Put it in a large saucepan with the onions, cover with water and bring quickly to the boil. After 5–6 minutes reduce the heat, add the seasoning and the bay leaf, cover with a lid and cook gently for 1½ hours. Add the sliced potatoes, and a little more hot water if necessary, and continue to cook until both meat and potatoes are well cooked. Remove from the heat. Beat the egg yolks with the lemon juice and gradually add 2–3 tablespoons of the hot liquid from the pan, beating all the while. Pour the egg mixture back into the pan and return to the heat for 2–3 minutes to bind the sauce, without letting it boil again. Pour into a sauce boat and sprinkle the chopped parsley on top. Serve with the pork.

Hirino me selinoriza avgolemono

Pork with celeriac and egg and lemon sauce

6 SERVINGS

1 2-lb. leg of pork
2 oz. butter
2 chopped onions
2 tablespoons flour
salt and pepper
2 tablespoons chopped
  parsley

¼ pint white wine
hot water
1 lb. celeriac
2 egg yolks
2 tablespoons lemon
  juice

Wipe the meat with a damp cloth and cut into 6 portions. Melt the butter in a large saucepan and fry the meat with the onions. Add the flour and mix well. Season to taste, add the chopped parsley and pour in the wine, and enough hot water to cover the meat completely. Scrape the celeriac, wash and cut into small pieces. Add to the meat and cook over gentle heat for 1½–2 hours, or until meat and celeriac are very tender. Beat the egg yolks with the lemon juice and gradually add 2–3 tablespoons of the hot liquid from the pan, beating all the while. Pour the egg mixture back into the pan and return to the heat for 2–3 minutes to thicken sauce, without letting it boil again. Pour into a dish and sprinkle the chopped parsley on top. Serve separately with the pork.

Nefra me saltsa

Kidneys in wine sauce

4 SERVINGS

½ oz. butter	1 bay leaf
1 tablespoon flour	salt and pepper
¼ pint red wine	1 lb. lambs' kidneys
3–4 tablespoons stock	2 oz. butter
or water	1 dozen button
1 clove garlic	mushrooms
½ teaspoon marjoram	juice ½ lemon
or thyme	

First make the sauce. Melt ½ the butter in a saucepan, add the flour and cook until light brown, stirring constantly. Pour in the wine gradually and stir in the stock, finely chopped garlic, marjoram, bay leaf and seasoning. Put over low heat and simmer for 15 minutes. Strain and return to the pan. Skin and remove the core from the kidneys, cut in four, and sprinkle with lemon juice. Melt the 2 oz. butter, and when hot lightly fry the kidneys and the mushrooms. When ready drop them in the sauce, but do not allow them to boil.

Sykoti tiganito

Liver fried in batter

4 SERVINGS

4 oz. flour
2 teaspoons baking
powder
1 teaspoon salt
1 egg
¼ pint milk and water
(approximately)

1½ lb. pigs' liver
boiling water
seasoned flour
fat for frying

Sift flour, baking powder and salt. Make a well in the middle and add the lightly beaten egg and milk and water mixture. Beat well for a few minutes and leave aside. Cut the liver into small pieces, put these in a basin and cover with boiling water. After 5 minutes drain well and remove the skin. Dip in seasoned flour, then in the batter, and deep fry in smoking hot fat until golden brown.

Glossa vodini braisé

Braised ox tongue

4–6 SERVINGS

1 medium-sized
ox tongue
water
salt and peppercorns
4 tablespoons butter
1 onion
2 carrots

2 sticks celery
6 tablespoons dry
white wine
1 lb. peeled tomatoes
1 small piece
cinnamon
3 cloves

Boil the ox tongue for 2–3 minutes and throw away the water. Rinse and return to the pan with enough hot water to cover. Add salt and peppercorns and simmer for about 2 hours. Remove the tongue from the stock and drop in a basin of cold water. Skin and remove the bones at the root. Heat the butter in a saucepan and brown the tongue all over. Transfer to a dish and add the onions, carrots and celery and cut into very small pieces. Fry for 5 minutes and place the tongue on the bed of vegetables. Pour in the wine and add the finely chopped tomatoes, and 2–3 tablespoons of the stock in which the tongue was boiled. Adjust the seasoning and add the cinnamon and cloves. Cover the pan and simmer gently for 35–40 minutes.

Sikotakia tis scaras

Grilled lamb's liver

4 SERVINGS

8 slices lamb's liver	$\frac{1}{2}$ teaspoon thyme
4 tablespoons olive oil	or marjoram
salt and pepper	1 tablespoon lemon juice

Wash the liver slices and wipe dry. Brush well with olive oil and grill, not too near the heat, turning once. Sprinkle with salt, pepper and marjoram or thyme. Mix the oil with the lemon juice and when well blended pour over the liver slices while hot. Serve immediately.

Sikotakia me saltsa spanaki

Liver with spinach sauce

4 SERVINGS

1 lb. calf's liver
seasoned flour
1 egg
3-4 tablespoons
  breadcrumbs olive
3-4 tablespoons olive
  oil
1 finely chopped small
  onion

1 crushed clove garlic
$\frac{1}{4}$ pint hot stock
  or water
1 teaspoon lemon juice
2 tablespoons chopped
  parsley
2 tablespoons chopped
  spinach
salt and pepper

Cut the liver in slices. Dip in seasoned flour, then in the beaten egg, and coat with breadcrumbs. Heat the olive oil in a pan, drop in the liver and fry quickly until brown. Remove on to a dish and keep warm. Add the chopped onion and crushed garlic to the pan and fry for a few minutes, add the stock and lemon juice and bring to the boil. Add the parsley and spinach, and season to taste. Boil for 5-6 minutes and pour over the liver slices.

Loukanika me saltsa

Frankfurters in wine sauce

4-6 SERVINGS

1 lb. frankfurter
  sausages
boiling water
2 tablespoons butter
2 tablespoons tomato
  purée
little water

2 skinned and chopped
  tomatoes
$\frac{1}{4}$ pint red wine
salt and pepper
pinch sugar
cooked rice or mashed
  potatoes

Plunge the frankfurters in boiling water and leave for 2-3 minutes. Pat dry and gently fry in the butter.

Remove sausages on to a dish. Dilute the tomato purée in a very little water and add to the pan, with the finely chopped tomatoes, wine, salt, pepper and sugar. Cook slowly for about 10 minutes. Cut each sausage into 3 pieces and drop into the sauce to warm through. Serve with either rice or mashed potatoes.

Sikotakia marinata

Marinated liver

4 SERVINGS

1 lb. lamb's or calf's liver	2 tablespoons vinegar
well seasoned flour	1 teaspoon tomato purée
olive oil for frying	$\frac{1}{4}$ pint water
2 tablespoons olive oil	few leaves rosemary
2 tablespoons flour	salt and pepper

Cut the liver in slices 1×2 inches long. Wash, dry and dip in well seasoned flour. Shallow fry in hot olive oil until both sides are well browned. Do not overcook. Remove liver and place in deep dish. Add the two tablespoons of oil into the frying pan, gradually stir in the flour, and keep stirring with a wooden spoon until the flour turns nut brown and the mixture is smooth. Add the vinegar little by little, the water in which you have diluted the tomato purée, and rosemary leaves, stirring all the time. Season to taste and let it simmer gently for 5–6 minutes. Pour the sauce over the liver slices and let it get cold. This dish is eaten cold and will keep for 3–4 days even without a refrigerator.

Note:

The point to be stressed here is that only olive oil should be used for frying. Butter or any other fat is not suitable.

Roulo me kima voliotiko

Meat roll (Volos style)

4 Servings

4 sheets phyllo pastry	pinch nutmeg
8 oz. minced meat	1 teaspoon chopped
1 chopped onion	parsley
4 oz. melted butter	$1\frac{1}{2}$ oz. flour
2 tablespoons dry	$\frac{1}{2}$ pint hot milk
red wine	2 tablespoons grated
1 teaspoon tomato purée	cheese
2 tablespoons water	1 egg yolk
salt and pepper	

Fry the minced meat and onion in 2 tablespoons of the melted butter. Add the wine, tomato purée, diluted previously in the water, salt, pepper and chopped parsley. Simmer covered until there is no liquid left. In the meantime, put 2 tablespoons of the butter in a small saucepan, add the flour and cook over low heat for a couple of minutes. Gradually add the hot milk, stirring continuously. Add nutmeg and more seasoning and continue to cook until the sauce thickens. Remove from the heat and stir in the grated cheese and beaten egg yolk. The sauce should be fairly stiff. Brush the pastry sheets with melted butter and place one on top of the other. Spread the sauce on top and cover with the minced meat mixture. Roll up lightly like a Swiss roll and place on a greased baking tray. Sprinkle over a few drops of water and score lightly into serving portions. Bake in a moderate oven until golden brown — about 30–35 minutes.

Moussakas patates

Potato moussaka

6 SERVINGS

1½ oz. butter
1 lb. minced meat
2 chopped onions
fat for frying
¼ pint wine
1 tablespoon tomato
    purée
little water
1 tablespoon chopped
    parsley
salt and pepper
3 large potatoes

5–6 tomatoes
2 tablespoons seasoned
    flour
1 egg yolk
½ pint white sauce
    (see page 195)
pinch nutmeg
2 tablespoons grated
    cheese
4 tablespoons toasted
    breadcrumbs

Melt 1 oz. of the butter, add the minced meat and onions and fry until brown. Stir in the wine, tomato purée previously diluted in a little water, parsley and seasoning. Cover the pan and cook gently for 30–40 minutes. While the meat is cooking gently, peel, slice and shallow fry the potatoes. Remove on to a plate. Cut the tomatoes in thick slices, dip in seasoned flour and fry quickly. Grease a pie dish well and cover the bottom with a layer of potatoes. Spread half the meat mixture on top and arrange a layer of tomato slices. Continue in this way until all the ingredients are used up, finishing with a layer of potatoes. Beat the egg yolk into the béchamel sauce and add a pinch of nutmeg. Spread this evenly on the potatoes and sprinkle thickly with the cheese and breadcrumbs. Pour over rest of butter and bake in a moderate oven for 30 minutes.

Note:

Instead of potatoes, you can use sliced marrow or pumpkin.

Moussakas melidzanes

Aubergine moussaka

6–7 SERVINGS

6–7 medium-sized aubergines	salt and pepper
1 oz. butter	6 tablespoons toasted breadcrumbs
1 lb. minced meat	$\frac{1}{4}$ pint olive oil for frying
2 chopped onions	2 egg yolks
$\frac{1}{4}$ pint dry red wine	$\frac{3}{4}$ pint white sauce
2 tablespoons tomato purée	(see page 195)
little water	2 tablespoons grated cheese
2 tablespoons chopped parsley	nut of butter

Remove the stalks from the aubergines and cut them lengthwise in slices $\frac{1}{4}$ inch thick. Sprinkle with salt and leave aside for 30 minutes or longer.

Melt the 1 oz. of butter, add the minced meat and onions and fry until brown. Stir in the wine, tomato purée previously diluted in a little water, parsley and seasoning. Cover the pan and cook gently for 30–40 minutes. Remove from the heat, add 4 tablespoons toasted crumbs and stir well. Rinse and wipe the aubergines dry. Heat the olive oil and fry the aubergine slices until golden on both sides. Grease a large ovenproof dish and sprinkle in 1 tablespoon breadcrumbs. Divide the aubergine slices in three portions. Arrange one layer in the dish and cover with half the minced meat, then the second layer of aubergines and the rest of the meat. Cover with the remaining aubergines. Beat the 2 egg yolks and stir into the béchamel sauce with 1 tablespoon of the cheese. Spread this on top of the aubergines, to cover the dish completely. Sprinkle the rest of the cheese and breadcrumbs and dot with the nut of butter. Bake in a moderate oven for 30 minutes or until the surface is golden brown.

This dish can be prepared well in advance and baked just before meal-time.

Roulo kima me domata

Meat loaf cooked in tomato sauce

1½ lb. lean pork	salt and pepper
1 thick slice toasted bread	1 egg
¼ pint milk	2 hard-boiled eggs
1 tablespoon finely chopped onion	flour
	2 oz. butter or margarine
1 tablespoon chopped parsley	4 peeled tomatoes
	4 tablespoons white wine
½ teaspoon sage	

Put the pork through a mincer twice. Soak the toast in the milk, mash well and add to the mince. Mix in the onion, parsley, sage and seasoning and bind with one lightly beaten egg. Turn the mixture on to a well floured board and pat to an oblong. Slice the hard-boiled eggs and arrange in the middle of the oblong lengthwise. Fold mixture round to seal the edges. Put the meat loaf in a roasting tin with the melted butter and bake in a moderate oven until nicely brown. Rub the tomatoes through a sieve and add to the tin. Pour in the wine and continue baking for a further 40 minutes.

Phyllo ya kreatopita

Pastry for meat pies

1 lb. flour	1 egg
1 teaspoon salt	warm water
3 tablespoons olive oil	

Sieve flour and salt into a bowl, make a well in the middle and add the olive oil. Gradually mix in the lightly beaten egg and enough warm water to form a soft dough. Knead the dough thoroughly for at least 10 minutes and leave in a cold place or a refrigerator to rest for 1 hour. Turn the dough on to a lightly floured pastry board and roll out to a thickness of less than ⅛ inch. Use as required.

Keftedes me saltsa

Meat balls in sauce

6 SERVINGS

Sauce:

4 oz. stale bread
4–5 tablespoons wine
1½ lb. finely minced steak
2 cloves garlic
salt and pepper
½ teaspoon wild
  marjoram or thyme
2 eggs
flour
fat for frying

1 small chopped onion
2 tablespoons butter
1 tablespoon flour
1 tablespoon tomato
  purée
scant ½ pint water
salt and pepper
pinch sugar

Remove the crust and soak the bread in the wine, until completely absorbed. Add to the minced steak, with the crushed garlic, salt, pepper and thyme or marjoram, and bind with the beaten eggs. Knead the mixture well and leave aside for 20–30 minutes. Should it be rather moist, add a very little flour. Form into small sausages and shallow fry until well browned. In the meantime make the sauce. Fry the chopped onion in the butter and add the flour, stirring with a wooden spoon until it turns brown. Dilute the tomato purée in water, add salt, pepper and sugar and pour into the pan. Cover and simmer for 10–15 minutes. Add the vinegar. When the meat balls are ready drop them in the sauce and simmer very gently for a further 5 minutes.

Kreatopita

Meat pie

6 SERVINGS

3 tablespoons melted
   butter
1½ lb. cooked minced meat
1 large onion, minced
3 eggs
1 tablespoon toasted
   breadcrumbs
chopped parsley

3 tomatoes
salt and pepper
pinch sugar

Pastry:

6 oz. flour
pinch salt
4 oz. butter or margarine
water to mix

Sieve the flour with the salt and rub in the butter. Add the water gradually to bind the pastry and roll out to ¼ inch thickness. Line a fairly deep fireproof dish with the pastry, prick the bottom well and leave in a cold place. Fry meat and onion lightly in 2 tablespoons butter. Remove from the heat, season well and mix in the lightly beaten eggs, breadcrumbs and a little chopped parsley. Empty the filling in the pastry case and spread evenly. Peel and half the tomatoes and arrange them on top of the meat mixture. Sprinkle with salt, pepper, sugar and the rest of the melted butter. Bake in a moderate oven for 30 minutes.

Keftedes tou fournou

Baked meat balls

6 SERVINGS

2 thick slices bread	2 large eggs
2 lb. finely minced chuck steak	1 tablespoon wine flour
1 large chopped onion	6 tablespoons melted butter
3 tablespoons chopped parsley	2 tablespoons lemon juice
1 teaspoon thyme	
salt and pepper	

Remove the crusts and soak the bread in cold water. Squeeze dry and add to the minced meat. Mix in the onion, parsley, thyme, seasoning, eggs and wine, until all the ingredients are well blended. Leave for 30 minutes. Shape the mixture into balls on a floured board, flatten slightly and arrange on a greased baking dish. Pour the melted butter and lemon juice over them and bake in a moderate oven until golden brown, basting occasionally with the liquid in the dish.

Krokettes me kreas

Meat croquettes

6–7 SERVINGS

1 lb. cooked meat	nutmeg
4 oz. ham	salt and pepper
2 oz. mushrooms	flour
8 oz. very stiff white sauce (see page 195)	2–3 tablespoons toasted crumbs
2 eggs	fat for frying

Chop the meat, ham and mushrooms into very small pieces. Make the béchamel sauce, and when cool beat in 1 egg yolk and a good pinch of nutmeg. Stir in the meat, ham and mushrooms and seasoning. Mix until all the ingredients are well blended. When the mixture is quite cold and firm, drop one tablespoonful at a time on to a well floured board and shape into a sausage. Beat 1 egg with 1 tablespoon water, dip in the croquettes and roll in the toasted crumbs. Deep fry in smoking hot fat for 1–2 minutes, or until golden colour. Drain on kitchen paper and serve hot.

Kreas krio gratin

Cold meat au gratin

4–5 SERVINGS

½ pint thick white sauce (see page 195)	3 hard-boiled eggs, sliced
salt and pepper	4 oz. grated cheese
1 tablespoon chopped parsley	4 tablespoons toasted breadcrumbs
1½ lb. cooked lamb or veal, sliced	2 oz. melted butter

Prepare the béchamel sauce, season well and stir in the chopped parsley. Butter a fireproof dish and spread a thin layer of sauce. Arrange on it half the meat and egg slices and sprinkle these with grated cheese. Add some more sauce and the rest of the meat and egg slices, and lastly a thick layer of sauce. Sprinkle with the rest of the cheese, the breadcrumbs and the melted butter. Cook in a hot oven for 10–15 minutes, or until the surface is golden brown.

Poultry and Game

The Sunday joint is not as common in Greece as it is in England. More often than not, chicken or some other special dish takes its place. The chicken is treated according to its age. A young plump bird is stuffed with a variety of mixtures and roasted, whereas an older bird is turned into a *stifado*, a pie or a fricassée. However, all birds and game alike are first given the lemon treatment—they are rubbed all over with lemon juice or a cut lemon. This not only keeps the flesh white, but improves the flavour. 'High' game is not popular. As in England turkey is eaten at Christmas, and I remember an old Greek pushing nuts down the bird's throat 'to make him fatter and tastier' for the Christmas table.

Kotopita

Chicken pie

8 SERVINGS

Filling:

1 boiling fowl
2 large onions, chopped
water
3 eggs
4 oz. grated cheese
salt and pepper
nutmeg
$\frac{1}{4}$ pint milk

Pastry:

1 lb. flour
salt
2 eggs
milk and water to mix
1 tablespoon melted
butter

Put the chicken in a saucepan and barely cover with water. Bring to the boil, skim well and add the coarsely chopped onions and salt to taste. Cover the saucepan and simmer until the meat comes away from the bones. (The time depends on the size and age of the bird.) Remove the chicken to a plate and cut into very small pieces, but continue to boil the onions until reduced to a thick pulp. Add the milk and the chicken pieces to the onion pulp and cook for a further 10 minutes. Remove the pan from the heat and cool slightly before adding the eggs, cheese and seasoning to taste. Mix with a wooden spoon until all the ingredients are thoroughly blended.

While the chicken is cooking prepare the pastry. Sift the flour with the salt into a basin. Make a well in the middle and add the eggs and the milk and water, little by little. Stir quickly with a fork and when well blended and easy to handle put on to a floured board, knead lightly with your fingertips and roll out about $\frac{1}{2}$ inch thick. Grease a shallow pie dish, line with the pastry, brush this with half the melted butter and pour in the chicken mixture. Cover with the remaining pastry and brush again with butter. Bake in a moderate oven for 45–50 minutes.

Kotopoulo yemisto

Stuffed chicken

6–8 SERVINGS

1 4-lb. chicken
1 tablespoon chopped
onion
2 oz. butter
salt and pepper
2 tablespoons brandy
4 oz. ground almonds

2 oz. ground walnuts
2 tablespoons chopped
parsley
3 tablespoons toasted
breadcrumbs
2 eggs
cinnamon (optional)

Chop the chicken liver, mix with the onion and fry lightly in half the butter until they begin to colour. Season well, pour in the brandy and simmer gently for 5 minutes. Mix in a basin the almonds, walnuts, parsley and breadcrumbs and add the fried onions. Bind with the lightly beaten eggs, adjust the seasoning and add a pinch of cinnamon if used. Stuff the chicken with the mixture and rub well with the rest of the butter. Place the chicken on a trivet in a roasting tin and cook in a moderate oven for 1 hour.

Kotopoulo me karydia (1)

Chicken in walnut sauce

6 SERVINGS

1 young chicken
4 oz. butter
2 chopped onions
2 tablespoons flour
salt and pepper

water
1 egg yolk
2 teaspoons cornflour
$\frac{1}{4}$ pint milk
4 oz. ground walnuts

Melt the butter in a saucepan and sauté the onions. Add the chicken, cut into six serving portions, and continue frying for 10 minutes. Stir in the flour, salt and pepper and enough water to barely cover the chicken. Cover the pan with a lid and simmer gently until the chicken is tender. Remove to a warm dish and bring the stock to the boil. Beat the egg yolk, mix in the cornflour and milk and pour into the pan, stirring continuously until the sauce comes to the boil again. Boil for 2–3 minutes and mix in the walnuts. Pour the sauce over the chicken and serve hot.

Kotopoulo me karydia (2)

Chicken in walnut sauce

4-6 SERVINGS

2 1½lb. chickens	⅛ pint hot water
4 oz. butter	salt and pepper
¼ pint dry white wine	2 oz. ground walnuts

Heat the butter in a frying pan and cook the chicken until golden brown all over. Transfer to a skillet, pour over the butter left in the pan, the wine and hot water. Cover with a lid and simmer gently until the birds are tender, adding a little more hot water if required, and seasoning to taste. Remove the birds on to a dish and cut into serving portions. Stir the walnuts into the sauce and boil for 1–2 minutes. Spread the sauce over the chicken and serve.

Poulia skaras

Grilled chicken

4 SERVINGS

1 young chicken
salt and pepper
2 tablespoons melted
butter

2 tablespoons toasted
breadcrumbs

Wipe the chicken and cut into four portions. Flatten with a wooden mallet or a rolling pin. Sprinkle with salt and pepper, dip in the melted butter and cover thickly with the breadcrumbs. Leave for 5–10 minutes for the crumbs to stick well on to the meat and brush carefully with some more melted butter. Grill for 20 minutes, not too close to the heat, turning the pieces once during the process.

Kotta stifado (1)

Chicken with onions

6–8 SERVINGS

1 3–4 lb. chicken
seasoned flour
2–3 tablespoons olive oil
40 shallots or small
   onions
2 oz. butter

$\frac{1}{4}$ pint wine
2 cloves garlic
1 bay leaf
salt and pepper
tomato purée
   (optional)

Wash and dry the chicken. Cut in suitable pieces for serving, dip in seasoned flour and fry in the olive oil until golden brown. Fry the onions whole in the butter, remove and place in a saucepan. Place the chicken pieces over the onions, pour in the wine and add the garlic, bay leaf, salt and pepper, and tomato purée if used. Cover well and cook over very low heat for about 45 minutes.

Kotta stifado (2)

Chicken with onions

6 SERVINGS

1 3-lb. chicken
4 oz. butter
40 small onions
2 tablespoons olive oil
2 tablespoons brandy

2 cloves garlic
1 bay leaf
¼ pint red wine
salt and pepper

Melt the butter in a saucepan and sauté the onions whole. Cut the washed and dried chicken into 6 portions and fry in the olive oil until golden brown all over. Place the chicken pieces on the onions, pour the brandy on top and set it alight. When the flames have subsided add the garlic, bay leaf, wine and seasoning. Cover the saucepan tightly and cook over gentle heat 45 minutes.

Kotopoulo katsarolas

Chicken pot roast

6 SERVINGS

1 medium-sized chicken
salt and pepper
pinch marjoram

4 oz. butter
juice 1 large lemon
¼ pint hot water

Rub the chicken with salt, pepper and marjoram. Heat the butter in a large saucepan and when smoking hot lower in the chicken and fry until golden on all sides. Pour in the lemon juice and simmer for 2–3 minutes. Add the water gradually, cover the pan tightly and cook very gently for about 1 hour, or until tender.

Mila yemista me kotta

Apples stuffed with chicken

4 Servings

1 breast of chicken
1 oz. melted butter
4 cloves
4 large cooking apples

1 tablespoon sugar
1 tablespoon toasted
  breadcrumbs
knob of butter

Mince the breast only of a steamed or boiled chicken
and mix with the melted butter and cloves. Cut the tops
off 4 even-sized apples, core and stuff with the mixture.
Place on a baking tray, sprinkle over the sugar and
breadcrumbs and dot with the butter. Cook in a moderate
oven until the apples are soft, but not mushy.

Kotopoulo me hilopites

Chicken with noodles

6 Servings

1 3–3½-lb. chicken
salt and pepper
4 tablespoons butter
2 chopped onions
2 crushed cloves garlic
¼ pint dry white wine
1 lb. peeled, sliced
  tomatoes
1 tablespoon tomato
  purée

½ pint hot water
4 tablespoons chopped
  celery
2 tablespoons chopped
  parsley
¼ teaspoon cinnamon
1 lb. noodles
3–4 tablespoons grated
  cheese

Cut the chicken into serving portions, sprinkle with salt
and pepper and fry in butter until golden brown. Remove
the chicken joints on to a hot dish and add the onion
and garlic to the fat in the pan. Fry until they begin
to colour and return the chicken on top of the onions.
Add the wine, tomatoes, tomato purée diluted in about

½ pint hot water, celery, parsley, cinnamon and seasoning. Cover the pan tightly and simmer until the chicken is tender. In the meantime bring 3 pints water to the boil with 1 tablespoon salt and throw in the noodles. Cook uncovered for 10–15 minutes. Drain thoroughly and put in a serving dish. Pour the sauce over the noodles and place the chicken joints on top. Sprinkle with cheese and serve immediately.

Papia me bamies

Duck with ladies' fingers

6 SERVINGS

1 young duck	1 teaspoon sugar
1 lb. ladies' fingers (okra)	3 tablespoons tomato purée
2 tablespoons vinegar	¼ pint hot stock or water
4 oz. butter	4 tablespoons dry white wine
flour	
salt and pepper	

Wash the ladies' fingers and lightly pare the stem end without cutting into the flesh. Drop these in a bowl of cold water to which you have added the vinegar and leave to soak for 30 minutes. Prepare the duck and cut into serving portions. Heat the butter in a frying pan, dip the duck pieces in seasoned flour and fry until golden brown. Transfer to a casserole. Drain the ladies' fingers and arrange carefully around the duck. Sprinkle with salt, pepper and sugar and pour in the wine and tomato purée diluted in the hot stock or water. Cover the casserole and place in a moderate oven to cook for 1 hour, or until the duck and vegetables are tender.

Note:

If fresh ladies' fingers are unobtainable, canned ones can be used instead. Just turn them into a collander and rinse thoroughly before adding them to the casserole.

Papia me mila

Duck stuffed with apples

6 SERVINGS

1 duck
3 cooking apples
2 teaspoons sugar
 little water
1 oz. butter
1 small stick cinnamon

2 nuts butter
1 tablespoon sugar
3 tablespoons wine
 vinegar
salt and pepper

Clean, wash and truss the duck. Peel the apples and cut into small pieces. Cover with a little water, add the cinnamon and 2 teaspoons sugar and cook gently until reduced to a pulp. Stuff the duck with the apple pulp. Melt the 1 oz. butter in a skillet and when hot add the duck and fry until it turns golden brown all over. In the meantime, melt the 2 nuts of butter in a small pan, add the sugar and the vinegar, salt and pepper to taste. Boil for 5 minutes and pour over the duck. Cover tightly with a lid, lower the heat and cook gently for 40–50 minutes.

Hina yemisti

Roast stuffed goose

16-20 SERVINGS

1 10-lb. goose
2 lb. chestnuts
2 oz. butter
1 small onion
$\frac{1}{4}$ pint milk
1 tablespoon chopped
 parsley
2 tablespoons pine
 kernels

1 teaspoon cinnamon
salt and pepper
1 tablespoon sugar
3 medium-sized cooking
 apples
$\frac{1}{2}$ lemon

Wash and dry the goose. Peel the chestnuts and put in a saucepan with water to cover. Boil gently for 20 minutes or until the inner skins will come off easily. Heat 1 oz. butter and lightly fry the chopped onion. Pour in the milk and add the parsley, pine kernels, cinnamon and seasoning. Bring to the boil and add the skinned chestnuts. Simmer chestnuts until all the milk is absorbed, but do not let them go pulpy. In the meantime, peel the apples and cut them into small pieces. Melt the rest of the butter, add the sugar and the apples and cook for about 10 minutes. Mix with the chestnuts and when the mixture is cold stuff the prepared goose. Rub the goose with the cut lemon, sprinkle with salt and pepper and place on a trivet in a roasting tin. Cook in a moderate oven for about 3 hours depending on the age of the goose.

Ortykia sti souvla

Quails on skewers

4 SERVINGS

4 quails   1 tablespoon lemon juice
2 tablespoons olive oil   salt and pepper

Mix the olive oil and lemon juice in a small basin. Clean and truss the quails, sprinkle with salt and pepper and thread on skewers. Cook slowly under the grill, not too near the heat, turning occasionally for even cooking and basting with the oil and lemon mixture. Ideally the quails should be cooked over a charcoal fire.

Hina yemisti me kima

Roast goose stuffed with minced meat

6–8 SERVINGS

1 medium-sized goose
with liver and heart
salt and pepper
4 oz. butter
1 lb. minced meat
1 finely chopped onion
1 tablespoon tomato
purée

$\frac{1}{4}$ pint hot water
2 tablespoons chopped
parsley
2 cloves
1 small piece cinnamon
4 tablespoons toasted
crumbs
2 oz. pine kernels

Prepare the goose and sprinkle with salt and pepper inside
and out. Heat the butter in a saucepan and fry the minced
meat, onions and the finely chopped liver and heart of
the goose. Pour in the wine and the tomato purée diluted
in the hot water and stir in the parsley, cloves, cinnamon
stick and salt and pepper. Cover with a lid and simmer
until the meat is almost cooked and very little liquid
left. Add the crumbs and pine kernels and remove from
the heat. Discard the cloves and cinnamon before using
the stuffing.

Place the goose on a rack in the roasting tin and cook
in a moderate oven for 2–2$\frac{1}{2}$ hours, depending on the
size of the bird.

Galos yemistos

Roast stuffed turkey

12–16 SERVINGS

10–12 lb. turkey,
dressed, with liver
and heart
2–3 oz. butter
2 chopped onions
1 lb. minced lamb or veal
2 tablespoons tomato
purée
2–3 tablespoons water

$\frac{1}{4}$ pint wine
2 tablespoons pine
kernels
2 tablespoons currants
6 tablespoons toasted
breadcrumbs
salt and pepper
$\frac{1}{2}$ lemon

Heat the butter and fry the chopped onions. When they begin to colour add the minced lamb and the finely chopped heart and liver. Continue to fry until brown. Dilute the tomato purée in the 2–3 tablespoons water and add to the pan, also the wine, the parsley and the seasoning. Cover with a lid and simmer for 10 minutes. Add the pine kernels and the currants and cook for a further 5 minutes. Remove from the heat and mix in the toasted breadcrumbs. The mixture should not be too stiff. Wash and dry the turkey and rub well all over with salt and the cut lemon. Stuff the bird and place on a trivet in the roasting tin. Cook in a moderate oven allowing 25–30 minutes per pound.

Galopoula me koukounaria

Turkey stuffed with pine kernels

6–8 SERVINGS

1 10-lb. turkey, with giblets	1 tablespoon tomato purée
4 oz. butter	little hot water
1 chopped onion	4 tablespoons brandy
6 oz. pine kernels	salt and pepper
8 oz. minced pork	pinch cinnamon
1½ lb. minced veal	2–3 eggs
	½ lemon

Heat the butter in a saucepan and lightly fry the onion. Add the pine kernels, and when they begin to colour add the minced pork, veal and finely chopped liver, heart and gizzard of the bird. Stir with a fork and cook until nicely brown. Pour in the tomato purée previously diluted in a little hot water, and the brandy, and add salt, pepper and cinnamon to taste. Cover the pan with a lid and simmer gently for 30 minutes. Remove from the heat, cool slightly and mix in the lightly beaten eggs. The mixture should not be stiff. Prepare the turkey and sprinkle the inside with salt and pepper. Rub the outside with the cut lemon dipped in salt. Stuff the bird at both ends and place on a grill in a large roasting tin (in Greece they often use tender branches of a vine tree instead of a trivet) and cook in a moderate oven for 4 hours.

Perdika salmi

Salmi of partridge

4–6 SERVINGS

2 partridges, with livers	¼ pint wine
salt and pepper	⅛ pint hot water
3 oz. butter	slices fried bread
1 lemon	

Rub the prepared birds with salt and pepper. Heat the butter in a skillet and quickly brown the birds all over. Add the finely chopped livers and the lemon juice and cook until this has been absorbed. Pour in the wine and water, cover with a lid and simmer gently for 40 minutes to 1 hour, according to the size and age of the partridges. Remove and place on a plate. Cut each bird into 2–3 portions. Place each portion on a slice of fried bread and pour the sauce over them. If the sauce is rather thin, boil it for 1–2 minutes to reduce it.

Becatsa salmi

Salmi of woodcock

2–4 SERVINGS

2 woodcocks, with livers	$\frac{1}{3}$ pint red wine
salt and pepper	1 bay leaf
4 oz. butter	pinch allspice
3 sliced onions	

Prepare the birds and rub well with salt and pepper. Remove the livers. Heat the butter in a skillet and fry the woodcocks until golden brown. Remove on to a dish and brown the onions in the skillet. Pour in the wine and bring to the boil. Cut the birds in halves and place on top of the onions. Add the bay leaf, finely chopped livers and seasonings, cover the pan with a lid and cook gently until the birds are tender. Remove them on to a serving dish and keep warm. Rub the onions and sauce through a sieve, heat thoroughly and pour over the birds.

Agriopapia me pilafi

Wild duck with pilaf

6 SERVINGS

1 duck, with giblets	1 medium-sized onion
vinegar	1 clove garlic
2 pints water	$\frac{1}{4}$ pint dry white wine
salt and pepper	4–5 sprigs parsley
2 oz. butter	1 lb. Patna rice
4 tablespoons olive oil	knob butter

Prepare the duck, remove the liver, heart and gizzard, and wash well. Put the duck in a bowl and cover with a mixture of vinegar and water and leave to marinate for 3–4 hours. Dry well and sprinkle with salt and pepper. In a large saucepan heat $\frac{1}{2}$ the butter and 2 tablespoons olive oil and fry the duck until golden brown. Cover the pan, lower the heat and let the duck cook gently in its own juice until tender, adding a little water as required. Heat the rest of the butter and oil in a small pan and fry the finely chopped liver, heart, gizzard, onion and garlic. Add the wine and chopped parsley and season to taste. Cover the pan and simmer for 15–20 minutes, adding a little more wine, if needed. In the meantime, throw the rice in to a saucepan of fast boiling salted water and cook for 6–7 minutes. Lower the heat, cover the pan and cook slowly until the rice is tender and all the water absorbed. Stir lightly with a fork and mix in the nut of butter. Place the duck in the middle of a dish, surround with the rice and serve the sauce separately.

Pitsounia krassata

Pigeons in wine sauce

4 SERVINGS

4 young tender pigeons
salt and pepper
4 oz. butter
3 tablespoons tomato
  purée

little hot water
½ pint red wine
small piece cinnamon
1 teaspoon sugar
2 cloves

Prepare the pigeons and rub well with salt and pepper. Heat the butter in a skillet and fry the birds until golden brown. Remove and place on a dish and split them in two. Dilute the tomato purée in a little hot water and add to the pan with the wine, salt, pepper, cinnamon and cloves. Simmer for 2–3 minutes and add the pigeons. Cover the pan and cook gently until the pigeons are tender and the liquid is reduced to a thick rich sauce.

Pitsounia me domates

Pigeons with tomatoes

4 SERVINGS

4 young tender pigeons
salt and pepper
4 oz. butter

1 lb. small tomatoes
½ pint dry white wine
½ teaspoon sugar

Clean and truss the pigeons and sprinkle with salt and pepper. Heat the butter in a skillet and lightly brown the pigeons. Peel the tomatoes and arrange round the birds. Pour in the wine, add salt, pepper and sugar, and cover the pan tightly. Cook over low heat until the pigeons are tender, 20–30 minutes, according to age and size. Drain the birds and place on a dish and keep warm. Increase the heat and boil the liquid rapidly for a few minutes. Arrange the tomatoes round the pigeons and pour over the sauce.

Pitsounia me elies

Pigeons with green olives

4 SERVINGS

4 young pigeons
2 oz. butter
salt and pepper
1 bay leaf
½ pint dry red wine

1 small jar green olives
1 teaspoon flour
1 teaspoon melted
butter

Heat the butter and fry the pigeons until brown. Split
each bird in two and transfer to a saucepan. Add the
seasoning and bay leaf and cover with the wine. Simmer
gently until tender. Rinse the olives in hot water and
add to the pan. Boil for 2–3 minutes. Mix the flour with
the melted butter and strain on to it some of the stock
from the pan. Mix well and return to the pan to boil
for a further 5–6 minutes.

Kouneli stifado

Rabbit with onions

6 SERVINGS

1 young rabbit
vinegar
4 oz. butter and oil,
mixed
16 pickling onions

2 tablespoons seasoned
flour
½ pint dry white wine
2 bay leaves
parsley

Wash the rabbit in plenty of water and cut into serving
portions. Put on a plate and sprinkle with vinegar. Cover
with a lid and leave for at least one hour. Heat the butter
and oil and lightly fry the onions. Remove to casserole.
Dry the rabbit, dip in seasoned flour and brown quickly
in the butter and oil. Place on top of the onions in the
casserole. Add the flour to the fat in the pan and cook

until it turns brown. Pour in $\frac{1}{4}$ pint of wine and bring
to the boil. Strain on to the rabbit and add the bay leaves,
salt, pepper and the rest of the wine. Cover and cook in
a very moderate oven until both rabbit and onions are
very tender. Before serving sprinkle with finely chopped
parsley.

Kouneli me ladorigani

Rabbit in oil and marjoram sauce

6 SERVINGS

1 young rabbit	1 clove garlic
salt and pepper	$\frac{1}{4}$ pint olive oil
2 teaspoons marjoram	juice 2 lemons

Soak the rabbit in salted cold water for at least 3 hours.
Dry well and sprinkle with salt, pepper and marjoram.
Push the garlic inside the rabbit. Place it on a trivet in
a roasting tin, blend the olive oil with the lemon juice
and pour it over the rabbit. Bake in a moderate oven
for 2 hours, basting frequently with the liquid in the tin.

Lagos tou fournou

Hare casserole

8 SERVINGS

1 hare

Marinade:

1 small onion, sliced
2–3 pieces of carrot
2 sticks of celery
2 sprigs parsley
1 bay leaf
peppercorns
vinegar and water

2 tablespoons seasoned
flour
$\frac{1}{4}$ pint olive oil
1 large onion, sliced
$\frac{1}{2}$ pint dry white wine
2 tablespoons vinegar
salt and pepper
water

Joint the hare and put into a basin with the marinade vegetables, and enough vinegar and water to cover. Leave for 1–2 days or even longer. Remove the pieces from the marinade, dry well and dip in the seasoned flour. Heat the olive oil in a frying pan and shallow fry the hare until brown. Remove to an earthenware casserole and fry the onion in the same oil. Place these on top of the hare and pour in the wine, vinegar and just enough water to cover the pieces completely. Add the garlic, the bay leaf and seasoning, cover the casserole and cook in a moderate oven for 2–2$\frac{1}{2}$ hours.

Lagos me saltsa karydia

Hare in walnut sauce

6 SERVINGS

1 medium-sized hare
vinegar
water
¼ pint olive oil
seasoned flour
1 finely chopped onion
2 cloves garlic
2 tablespoons finely
  chopped celery

2 tablespoons finely
  chopped parsley
3 tablespoons finely
  chopped carrots
2 sprigs rosemary
2 bay leaves
salt and pepper
½ pint dry red wine
2–3 oz. walnuts, ground

Wash and joint the hare. Put in a jug and cover with a mixture of vinegar and water to marinate for a few hours. Dry the pieces thoroughly. Heat the oil in a frying pan, dip the hare in seasoned flour and fry until golden brown. Place the hare joints in a saucepan and add the chopped vegetables to the frying pan to cook for a few minutes. Cover the hare with the vegetables, add the rosemary, bay leaves and seasoning and pour in the wine. Cover the saucepan with a lid and cook over low heat for 2–2½ hours. Remove the joints to a platter and keep warm. Rub the vegetables through a sieve, stir in the walnuts and return to the heat. Boil for 1 minute and pour over the hare.

The Greek way of cooking vegetables is imaginative and very tasty. Needless to say, for the best results vegetables should be young, fresh and tender.

Like all the other Mediterranean countries Greece has a great wealth of vegetables throughout the year and most of these can now be bought in England, both imported or home-grown varieties.

It is to the Greeks that we owe the discovery of the many familiar vegetables of today. Since Homeric times vegetables have been prominent on the Greek menu even on festive occasions, not merely as an accompaniment to meat or fish but also as a separate dish in their own right. Wild vegetables and herbs also have a place in the Greek kitchen and the country folk still treat their ailments with the herbs they pick on the mountainside in preference to pills and tablets. Most of the herbs mentioned in this book can be grown in England, even in window boxes, and dill, which is so freely used in Greek dishes, is one of the nicest herbs I know.

Kolokithakia plaki

Courgettes with cheese

6 SERVINGS

2 lb. courgettes
¼ pint olive oil
1 lb. fresh or canned
   tomatoes, drained
2 tablespoons chopped
   parsley

3–4 cloves garlic
salt and pepper
6 oz. cheese

Cut the courgettes into rounds about ½ inch thick. Wash and dry thoroughly. Heat the olive oil in a frying pan and lightly fry the courgette rounds for 5–6 minutes, or until they begin to colour. Add the skinned and chopped tomatoes, parsley, garlic and seasoning. Cover with a lid and cook gently until the courgettes are tender. Transfer to an ovenproof dish, cover the surface with thin slices of cheese and pop into a hot oven to colour the top. This could be done under the grill, if preferred.

Dolmades me klimatophylla

Vine leaves stuffed with meat

6–7 SERVINGS

12 oz. vine leaves or 1 15-oz. can	1 tablespoon chopped dill or 1 teaspoon mint
1 lb. minced lamb or veal	salt and pepper
4 oz. rice	4 oz. butter
1 large chopped onion	juice $\frac{1}{2}$ lemon
1 tablespoon chopped parsley	yoghurt (optional)

First prepare the vine leaves. If fresh ones are being used, dip them in boiling water for 5–10 minutes to soften them. If canned or preserved in brine, just rinse them thoroughly in hot water and spread out on a large plate. Mix the mince with the rice, onion, parsley, dill or mint, and season well. Take one vine leaf with shiny side away from you and put one good teaspoonful of stuffing on the stalk end of the leaf. Roll up, tucking in the edges at the same time to form a neat little roll. Line a skillet with any torn or very small leaves and arrange the rolls close together. Cover with some more vine leaves and arrange a second row. Add the butter cut in small pieces, and the lemon juice, and pour in enough hot water to cover the dolmades completely. Press a plate on top to keep them well immersed in the liquid and cook gently for 45–60 minutes. These dolmades are eaten hot and preferably with yoghurt poured on top, allowing one tablespoon per person. The combination of flavours is very agreeable.

Note:

Vine leaves are available in 15-oz. cans containing 40–50 vine leaves, according to make.

Lahano dolmades

Cabbage stuffed with meat **(1)**

4–6 SERVINGS

1 medium-sized white cabbage	4 oz. rice
boiling water	salt and pepper
1 lb. minced pork or lamb	3 tablespoons butter
2 chopped onions	Egg and lemon sauce
1 tablespoon chopped dill, or parsley	(see page 194)

Cut off the stalk and put the cabbage in a large saucepan with boiling salted water to cover. Cook for about 10 minutes. Drain and cool under the cold water tap. Separate the leaves carefully and remove the coarse veins. Mix the minced meat with the chopped onions, dill or parsley, rice and seasoning. Put one spoonful of the mixture on each cabbage leaf and roll up like a cigar. Tuck the edges in as you roll and squeeze gently to make a neat little parcel — the size depending on the size of the leaves. Line a frying pan or fireproof dish with 2–3 leaves and arrange the dolmades in rows close together. Cut the butter in small pieces and add to the pan and enough hot water to cover. Adjust the seasoning and put a plate on top. Cover with a lid and simmer gently for 1 hour. Prepare the egg and lemon sauce with the liquid in the pan. Return to the heat for a few minutes to allow the sauce to thicken, but do not let it boil again. Serve hot.

Lahano dolmades

Stuffed cabbage leaves (2)

4–5 Servings

1 medium-sized white
   cabbage
boiling water
¼ pint olive oil
2 chopped onions
8 oz. rice
1 tablespoon chopped
   dill or parsley

2 tablespoons currants
2 tablespoons pine
   kernels
pinch sugar
pinch cinnamon
salt and pepper

Cut off the stalk and put the cabbage in a large saucepan
with boiling salted water to cover. Cook for about 10
minutes. Drain and cool under the cold water tap.
Separate the leaves carefully and remove the coarse
veins. Put half the oil in a saucepan and fry the onions
until just beginning to colour. Toss in the rice and add
½ pint boiling water, the dill, currants, pine kernels, sugar
and cinnamon. Season well with plenty of pepper. Stir
until all the ingredients are blended and bring to the boil.
Cover the pan with a lid, lower the heat and cook slowly
for 20 minutes. Stuff the prepared cabbage leaves with
the mixture, roll up into neat little parcels and arrange
in rows in a skillet. Pour in the rest of the oil, sprinkle
with more salt and pepper and add enough hot water
to cover completely. Cook gently for about 1 hour,
or until the cabbage is quite tender. These dolmades
are served cold.

Dolmades diaforoi

Stuffed vegetables

4 SERVINGS

4 medium-sized tomatoes	salt and pepper
4 small aubergines	1 tablespoon chopped
4 small courgettes	parsley
4 tablespoons butter	4 oz. rice
1 chopped onion	2 tablespoons toasted
12 oz. minced steak	breadcrumbs

Cut the tops off the tomatoes to form a lid and with a teaspoon scoop out the pulp and the seeds. Sprinkle a little salt inside and turn upside down on to a plate to drain. Cut off and discard the green end of the aubergine. Make a deep slit lengthwise and scoop out the flesh. Sprinkle the flesh and the aubergine shell with salt. Lightly scrape the skin of the courgettes and cut off the two ends. Using an apple corer remove pulp and seeds. Heat 2 tablespoons of butter in a saucepan and fry the chopped onion and minced steak until brown. Season well with salt and pepper and add the parsley and the pulp of the tomatoes, aubergines and courgettes. Cook over gentle heat for 20 minutes. Add the rice and cook for a further 5 minutes. Stuff the vegetables with this mixture and place them in a well greased fireproof dish. Melt the rest of the butter and mix with the toasted breadcrumbs. Spread the mixture on top of the vegetables and bake in a moderate oven for about 1 hour.

Domates yemistes me rizi

Tomatoes with rice stuffing

4 SERVINGS

6–8 large firm tomatoes
scant ¼ pint olive oil
2 finely chopped onions
3 oz. rice
3 tablespoons chopped parsley
1 heaped tablespoon currants

salt and pepper
5 tablespoons hot water
2 tablespoons dry breadcrumbs
3 parboiled potatoes

Cut the tops off the tomatoes to form a lid and scoop out the pulp. Force the pulp through a sieve. Sprinkle the inside of the tomatoes with salt and leave on a tray, cut side down, to drain well. Heat just under half the oil in a saucepan and lightly fry the onion and rice. Add half the tomato pulp, parsley, currants and seasoning and hot water. Cover the pan with a lid and simmer gently until the rice is partly cooked and there is no liquid left. Place the tomatoes in a shallow baking dish and fill them with the mixture. Place the lids on and pour over them the rest of the oil. Sprinkle the tops with the breadcrumbs and add the rest of the tomato pulp. Slice the half cooked potatoes and arrange between the tomatoes. Season and bake in a moderate oven for 40–45 minutes. This dish is eaten hot or cold.

Piperies yemistes

Stuffed green peppers

4–8 SERVINGS

6–8 large green peppers
3–4 tablespoons butter
1 lb. raw minced meat
1 large chopped onion
4 oz. rice

1 tablespoon chopped parsley
1 teaspoon chopped mint
salt and pepper
½ pint water

Slice off the stalk end and put aside to be used as a lid. De-seed the peppers and sprinkle the inside with salt. Heat the butter in a saucepan and lightly fry the minced meat and onion. Stir in the rice and add the parsley, mint, seasoning and water. Cover the pan and cook gently for 15 minutes, by which time the rice should have absorbed all the liquid. Pack the peppers with this mixture, replace the lid and arrange them in a shallow baking dish. Add 2–3 tablespoons water and bake in a moderate oven for 40 minutes. This dish can be cooked equally well on top of the cooker. Place the peppers in a saucepan, add a nut of butter and 3–4 tablespoons of water and cook over a low heat until tender.

Kounoupidi me avga

Cauliflower in cheese custard

4–5 SERVINGS

1 medium-sized cauliflower	3 eggs
butter or oil for frying	salt and pepper
flour	3 tablespoons grated cheese

Wash the cauliflower and separate into tiny flowerets. Parboil in a pan of boiling salted water and leave to drain well. Heat the butter or oil in a large frying pan, dip the cauliflower in the flour and fry lightly. Beat the eggs with the seasoning, add the grated cheese and pour over the cauliflower. Lower the heat and cook until the eggs are well puffed and set. Turn on to a warm dish and serve immediately.

Melidzanes imam baïldi

Aubergines Imam Bayildi (1)

This dish was introduced to Greece from Turkey and the name means 'the Imam fainted', the Imam being a Turkish priest. There is an anecdote explaining why he fainted. One version is that it was with sheer delight on tasting the dish which his loving wife had prepared for him. Another version is that the Imam was a poor and mean man, and when he worked out the cost of the olive oil in which the aubergines were swimming, he just passed out. Yet a third version of the same anecdote is — But I would rather give you the recipe, which caused the fainting fit and leave you to draw your own conclusions.

5 aubergines
1½ lb. sliced onions
1½ lb. chopped, peeled
  tomatoes
salt and pepper

2–3 cloves garlic
¾ pint olive oil
handful chopped
  parsley
pinch sugar

Cut off the stalk end of the aubergines and with a sharp knife make 3–4 slits lengthwise. Sprinkle a little salt inside the slits and stand aside for 15–20 minutes. Rinse the aubergines and squeeze gently to extract any excess water. Heat 2 gills olive oil and fry the aubergines until golden brown. Remove on to a plate and fry the sliced onions in the same pan. Mix the onions, garlic, tomatoes, parsley and seasoning, and when the aubergines are cool enough to handle press the slits open and stuff with the mixture. Put some of the stuffing on the bottom of a shallow baking dish, arrange the aubergines on top, cover with a few slices of tomatoes and pour over the rest of the olive oil. Sprinkle a little more salt and pepper and the sugar and bake in a moderate oven for 50–60 minutes, or until the aubergines are quite tender. This dish is always served cold.

Depending on the size of the aubergines, this quantity makes 3–5 servings.

Melidzanes imam baïldi

Aubergines Imam Bayildi (2)

3–5 SERVINGS

5 aubergines
2 sliced onions
4 tomatoes, peeled
 and chopped
¼ pint olive oil

4 tablespoons chopped
 parsley
salt and pepper
1 teaspoon sugar

Cut off the stalk end of the aubergines. Peel a strip about ½ inch wide on both sides and with a sharp knife slit right through, leaving the two ends intact. Sprinkle the inside with salt and leave aside for 15–20 minutes. Rinse and squeeze the aubergines to get rid of excess water and place in a skillet unpeeled side upwards. Mix the sliced onions with the chopped, peeled tomatoes and the parsley, add salt and pepper and moisten with 2 tablespoons olive oil. Stuff the aubergines with the mixture, sprinkle with salt, pepper and sugar and pour the rest of the oil on top. Add enough water to cover completely and cook over gentle heat for about 1 hour, or until the aubergines are quite soft. This dish can be served hot or cold.

Melidzana pouré

Aubergine purée

4–6 SERVINGS

4 medium-sized aubergines	4 tablespoons thin cream or hot milk
4 tablespoons butter	salt and white pepper

Bake the aubergines in a moderate oven until the skins turn brown and begin to blister (30–35 minutes), or grill very gently. As soon as they are cool enough to handle peel and scoop out the centre. Put the flesh, which should be soft and creamy, into a bowl and pound to a paste. Add the butter and cream or milk, season well and stir until thoroughly blended, then beat for a few minutes to make the mixture smooth and light. Reheat either over boiling water or put in an enamel pan. This purée is delicious with roast veal.

Briani nistisimo

Ragoût of mixed vegetables

4–6 SERVINGS

1 lb. potatoes	1 green pepper
salt and pepper	1 red pepper
1 tablespoon chopped dill	1 large onion
1 tablespoon chopped parsley	8 oz. string beans
3 finely chopped cloves garlic	4–5 tomatoes
2 large aubergines	8 tablespoons olive oil
4 courgettes	4 tablespoons water
	4 tablespoons dried breadcrumbs

Brush an earthenware casserole with oil and arrange a layer of sliced potatoes. Sprinkle with salt, pepper, dill, parsley and garlic and then a layer of cubed aubergines. Sprinkle these with seasoning and herbs and proceed in this way, arranging the various vegetables in layers. The courgettes should be lightly scraped and cut into rounds, the peppers de-seeded and sliced, and the onion, beans and tomatoes skinned and sliced. Add the olive oil and 4 tablespoons water, sprinkle the breadcrumbs on top and cook covered in a moderate oven for about 50 minutes.

Fassolia pouré

Butter bean purée

4–5 SERVINGS

1 lb. butter beans	2 cloves crushed garlic
3 pints water	salt and pepper
1 chopped onion	chopped parsley
2 potatoes	paprika
6 tablespoons olive oil	

Soak the beans overnight. Put in a large saucepan with the water and the onion and bring to the boil. Reduce the heat, cover the pan and simmer gently until the beans are almost cooked. Add the chopped potatoes and continue to cook until beans and potatoes are very soft. Rub through a sieve and return to the pan. Add the olive oil, crushed garlic, salt and pepper, and mix until all the ingredients are thoroughly blended. Turn on to a dish, arrange in a mound and decorate with the chopped parsley and paprika. This dish is delicious served with fried sausages or frankfurters.

Kolokithokeftedes

Courgette rissoles

6–8 SERVINGS

1½ lb. courgettes or
   vegetable marrow
1 egg
4 oz. toasted breadcrumbs
3 tablespoons grated
   cheese

chopped parsley
salt and pepper
1 finely chopped onion
   fried in butter
flour
fat for frying

Peel the courgettes or marrow and steam until very tender. Drain well and mash. Stir in the egg, breadcrumbs, cheese, parsley and seasoning. Add the fried onion to the other ingredients. Mix until well blended and shape into round flat cakes. Dip them in flour and shallow fry until golden brown.

Pastitsio Patata

Potato pie

6 SERVINGS

3 lb. potatoes
2 oz. butter
1 lb. freshly minced
   meat
1 large chopped onion
¼ pint tomato juice
2–3 tablespoons water
3 eggs

3 tablespoons grated
   cheese
nutmeg to taste
salt and pepper
2 tablespoons toasted
   breadcrumbs
1 tablespoon melted
   butter

Boil the potatoes in their skins. Peel and mash well or put through a 'mouli' sieve. While the potatoes are cooking, heat the butter in a pan and fry the minced meat and onion until brown. Add the tomato juice, salt and pepper and a few tablespoons water. Cover the pan with a lid and simmer for about 1 hour, depending on the meat you are using. There should be no liquid left. In the meantime beat 2 eggs into the mashed potatoes and add 2 tablespoons grated cheese, nutmeg and seasoning. Spread half the potato mixture in a greased baking dish, add the mince and cover with the rest of the potato. Beat the remaining egg and pour over the surface. Sprinkle with toasted crumbs, the rest of the cheese and the melted butter. Cook in a moderate oven for 30 minutes.

Patates yahni

Potato ragoût

1½ lb. potatoes	2 carrots, cut in small dice
4–5 tablespoons olive oil	
1 finely chopped onion	1 tablespoon finely chopped celery
3 fresh tomatoes, or canned	
2 cloves garlic, crushed	salt and pepper
	½ pint water

Peel the potatoes and cut in small chunks. Heat the olive oil in a saucepan and lightly fry the onion. Add the peeled and finely chopped tomatoes, the garlic, carrots, celery and seasoning to taste. Cover with the water and bring to the boil. Add the potatoes, cover the pan and cook over gentle heat until all the vegetables are cooked and there is very little liquid left.

Patates me rigani

Potatoes with marjoram

1½ lb. potatoes	4–5 tablespoons olive
salt and pepper	oil
marjoram or thyme	juice 1 lemon

Peel, wash and cut the potatoes in thick slices. Sprinkle with salt and pepper and arrange in a shallow ovenware dish. Sprinkle with marjoram or thyme to taste and pour over the oil and lemon juice. Bake in a moderate oven for 45–50 minutes. This dish can be served hot or cold.

Kounoupidi stiffado

Cauliflower with onions

6–8 SERVINGS

1 large cauliflower	¼ pint water
4 oz. olive oil	1 bay leaf
5 pickling onions	1 sprig rosemary
2 cloves garlic	salt and pepper
2 tablespoons tomato	2 tablespoons wine
purée	vinegar

Remove the leaves, cut off the stalk and separate the cauliflower into flowerets. Leave in cold water for 10–15 minutes. In the meantime heat the oil in a saucepan and lightly fry the onions and garlic. Dilute the tomato purée in the water and add to the pan with the bay leaf, rosemary, seasoning and vinegar. Cover and simmer for 30 minutes. Cook the cauliflower in boiling salted water for about 10 minutes (do not over-cook), drain well and add to the sauce, with a little more water if required. Simmer for a further 10–15 minutes, by which time the cauliflower should be quite tender and the sauce rich and thick.

Tyropita spanaki

Cheese and spinach tart

6–8 SERVINGS

1 oz. butter
1 oz. flour
¼ pint hot milk
salt and pepper
nutmeg
1 lb. spinach, cooked

3 eggs
4–6 oz. grated cheese
8 tablespoons meat stock
8 oz. phyllo pastry
6 tablespoons melted
butter

Melt the butter in a saucepan over low heat, add the flour and cook for 2–3 minutes, stirring all the while. Gradually pour in the hot milk and season to taste. Simmer until the sauce is thick and remove from the heat. Stir in the cooked and finely chopped spinach, the beaten eggs, cheese and meat stock. Butter a tin the size of the pastry (12 × 16 inches) and line with one sheet. Brush this with melted butter and add another sheet. Continue in this way until you have used half the pastry. Carefully spread the spinach mixture and cover with the rest of the pastry, brushing each sheet with melted butter, as before. With the point of a sharp knife divide the pastry into squares and bake in a moderate oven for 30–35 minutes.

Krokettes patatas

Potato croquettes

4 SERVINGS

1 lb. potatoes
1 tablespoon melted
butter
2 oz. grated cheese
1 egg yolk
salt and pepper

pinch nutmeg
1 beaten egg
flour
toasted breadcrumbs
olive oil for frying
chopped parsley

Boil the potatoes in their skins. Peel and mash until smooth, or put through a 'mouli' sieve, stir in the melted butter, cheese, egg yolk and seasoning. Mix thoroughly. Empty the mixture on to a floured pastry board and with floured hands roll out into a long 'sausage'. Cut into even-sized pieces, dip in beaten egg, roll in crumbs and deep fry in smoking hot oil until golden brown. Sprinkle with parsley and serve hot.

Patates me saltsa krema

Potatoes in white sauce

3–4 SERVINGS

1 lb. potatoes
1 oz. butter
1½ oz. flour
½ pint hot milk

salt and pepper
nutmeg to taste
chopped parsley

Boil the potatoes in their skins, but do not over-cook. Peel and slice. Melt the butter over low heat, add the flour and cook for 2–3 minutes, stirring continuously. Add the hot milk gradually, also the salt, pepper and nutmeg. Cook gently for 10 minutes and mix in the potatoes and parsley. Simmer for a further 4–5 minutes. Serve hot with chicken or any grilled meat.

Kolokithia yahni

Courgettes with onions and tomatoes

6 SERVINGS

2 lb. courgettes or marrow
¼ pint olive oil
3 chopped onions
1 lb. tomatoes

1 tablespoon chopped parsley
salt and pepper
little water

Lightly scrape the courgettes and cut into 1-inch squares. Heat the olive oil in a saucepan and fry the onions until golden brown. Add the peeled and finely chopped tomatoes, parsley, salt and pepper and a very little water. Bring to the boil and stir in the courgettes or marrow. Lower the heat, cover the pan and simmer gently until all the vegetables are cooked and the sauce is rich and thick.

Soufflé patates

Potato soufflé

6 SERVINGS

2 lb. potatoes
3 tablespoons melted butter
8 tablespoons warm milk
4 egg yolks

4 oz. grated cheese
salt and pepper
pinch nutmeg
4 egg whites

Boil the potatoes in their skins. Peel and rub through a sieve. Stir in the melted butter and milk and mix thoroughly. Add the lightly beaten egg yolks, the cheese, salt, pepper and nutmeg, and finely fold in the stiffly whipped egg whites. Turn the mixture into a well buttered fireproof dish and bake in a moderately hot oven for 25–30 minutes. Serve immediately.

Melidzanes 'Papoutsakia'

Aubergines 'Little Shoes'

6 SERVINGS

6 medium-sized
aubergines
oil for frying
4 oz. butter or margarine
8 oz. freshly minced meat
1 large chopped onion
6 peeled and finely
chopped tomatoes
4–5 tablespoons dry
white wine

salt and pepper
4 tablespoons grated
cheese
4 tablespoons dry
breadcrumbs
1 egg
½ pint white sauce
(see page 195)
hot water

Cut off the stalk and divide the aubergines in two lengthwise. Sprinkle with salt and leave for about 30 minutes. Rinse, dry well and lightly fry in oil until they begin to soften. Arrange the aubergines in a baking dish, scoop out the insides carefully and keep the pulp. Heat the butter in a saucepan and brown the minced meat and onion. Add the aubergine pulp, 3 finely chopped tomatoes, the wine and seasoning, and cook gently for 20–25 minutes. Remove from the heat and stir in 2 tablespoons grated cheese and 2 of breadcrumbs. Bind the mixture with the lightly beaten egg and fill the aubergines. Cover with the béchamel sauce and sprinkle the rest of the cheese and breadcrumbs on top. Rub the rest of the tomatoes through a sieve and add to the dish with 2–3 tablespoons hot water. Adjust the seasoning and bake in a moderate oven for 30 minutes.

Tiganites me karota

Carrot fritters

1 lb. carrots	salt and pepper
3 tablespoons butter	1 egg white
1 tablespoon flour	deep fat for shallow
1 egg yolk	frying
1 tablespoon brandy	lemon wedges

Scrape and cut the carrots into small pieces. Cook in salted boiling water for 15 minutes. Drain well and rub through a sieve. Stir in the butter and flour and mix thoroughly. Add the egg yolk, brandy and seasoning and fold in the stiffly beaten egg white. Drop spoonfuls of the mixture in the smoking hot fat and fry until golden brown. Drain and serve garnished with the lemon wedges.

Fassolia freska yahni

Runner beans with onions and tomatoes

4-6 SERVINGS

3–4 oz. butter	salt and pepper
3 chopped onions	2½ lb. runner or French
1 lb. tomatoes	beans
1 tablespoon chopped parsley	

Melt the butter in a saucepan and lightly fry the onions. Add the peeled and finely chopped tomatoes, parsley and seasoning, and bring to the boil. Trim and slice the beans, but not too finely, and add to the pan with enough water to cover the beans completely. Cover with a lid, lower the heat and simmer gently for 40–50 minutes until the beans are tender and the sauce is thick.

Melidzanes tiganites

Aubergine fritters

4–6 SERVINGS

4 large aubergines,
  unpeeled
salt
1 oz. flour

deep oil for frying
1 bottle yoghurt
1 clove garlic
(optional)

Cut the aubergines into long slices ¼ inch thick. Sprinkle
with salt and leave them to stand for 30–40 minutes,
to extract any water. Rinse, dry and dredge well with
flour. Fry in smoking hot oil until both sides are golden
brown. Drain on kitchen paper. They should be crisp
on the outside and soft and creamy inside. Serve hot
with cold yoghurt poured over them. If garlic is used
mash to a cream and add to the yoghurt before serving.

Melidzanes pane

Fried aubergines

4 SERVINGS

3 medium-sized
  aubergines
salt and pepper
2 eggs
2 tablespoons water
2 tablespoons flour

3 tablespoons grated
  Parmesan cheese
2 tablespoons dry
  breadcrumbs
oil for frying

Cut the aubergines in long slices about ¼ inch thick.
Sprinkle with salt and leave for 30 minutes. Rinse and
dry well. Beat the eggs with 2 tablespoons water. Mix
the flour with the Parmesan or any other cheese you
are using. Dip the aubergine slices first in the flour-
cheese mixture, then in the egg, and cover with the
crumbs. Fry in smoking hot oil until crisp and golden
brown on both sides.

Domates yemistes me melidzana

Tomato and aubergine savoury

3–4 SERVINGS

2 medium-sized aubergines	4 tablespoons grated cheese
6–8 large firm tomatoes	6 tablespoons dry breadcrumbs
6 tablespoons olive oil or melted butter	1 tablespoon chopped parsley
1 tablespoon chopped onion	salt and pepper
little flour	2 hard-boiled eggs
2 oz. rice	little water

Peel the aubergines, cut into small dice and drop in a basin of cold salted water. Wash the tomatoes, cut off the top and scoop out the pulp. Sprinkle the inside of the tomatoes with salt and turn upside down on to a plate to drain. Force the pulp through a sieve. Heat the oil or butter and lightly fry the onion. Dry the aubergines, dip in flour and fry with the onion until golden brown. Remove from the heat and stir in the rice, cheese, breadcrumbs, parsley and seasoning. Add half the tomato pulp and mix thoroughly. Fill the tomatoes with the mixture and top with a slice of hard-boiled egg. Arrange in a shallow baking dish close together, add the rest of the tomato pulp and very little water, if necessary, and bake in a moderate oven for 30–40 minutes.

Domates me kima

Tomatoes stuffed with minced meat

5 SERVINGS

10 large firm tomatoes
4 oz. butter
2 chopped onions
1 lb. very finely minced chuck steak
4 tablespoons wine
2 tablespoons chopped parsley

1 tablespoon chopped dill
salt and pepper
$\frac{1}{8}$ pint water
5 tablespoons grated cheese
5 tablespoons toasted crumbs

Slice off the top of the tomatoes and put aside. Scoop out the pulp and force through a sieve. Sprinkle the tomatoes with salt and turn upside down on to a plate to drain. Heat 2 oz. butter in a pan and fry the onions and minced meat until brown. Add the wine, tomato pulp, parsley, dill and seasoning, and pour in the water. Simmer for 30–40 minutes, or until the meat has absorbed all the liquid. Remove the pan from the heat and mix in the grated cheese and breadcrumbs. When all the ingredients are well blended put one good dessert-spoonful of the mixture in each tomato and cover with the cut-off slice. Arrange the tomatoes close together in a shallow baking dish. Melt the rest of the butter and pour over the tomatoes. Bake in a moderate oven for 30–35 minutes.

Melidzanes ragou

Aubergine ragoût

4–6 SERVINGS

2 lb. lamb or veal
2 oz. butter
3 medium-sized chopped onions
3 chopped peeled tomatoes
1 tablespoon tomato purée

½ pint water
salt and pepper
2 tablespoons chopped parsley
4 aubergines
1 teaspoon cornflour
1 tablespoon water

Wipe the meat with a damp cloth and cut into serving portions. Heat the butter in a large saucepan and brown the meat and the onions. Add the peeled, chopped tomatoes, the tomato purée diluted in ½ pint water, and salt and pepper to taste. Cover the pan and cook slowly for 30 minutes. In the meantime, cut the aubergines in thick rounds, sprinkle with salt and leave aside for 10–15 minutes. Rinse and add to the meat together with the chopped parsley and some more salt and pepper. Put a plate on top of the aubergines to keep them immersed in the liquid, cover the pan with a lid and simmer until the aubergines are quite soft. Dilute the cornflour in a spoonful of water and add to the pan. Boil for a further 2 minutes to thicken.

Selinoriza tiganiti

Fried celeriac

4–6 SERVINGS

2 large celeriac
4 oz. sifted flour
salt and pepper
1 teaspoon olive oil
4 tablespoons white wine
   or beer

4 tablespoons water
1 egg white
deep oil for frying
1 tablespoon grated
   cheese

Wash and peel the celeriac roots. Cut into slices about
$\frac{1}{4}$ inch thick and drop in some boiling salted water. Boil
gently for 20 minutes and strain. In the meantime mix
the flour with the salt, pepper and olive oil and gradually
add the wine and water. Beat well. Whip the egg white
until stiff and fold in. Dip the celeriac slices in the batter
and drop in the smoking hot oil. Fry until golden brown.
Drain on kitchen paper, and serve at once with the
cheese sprinkled on top.

Spanakorizo

Spinach with rice

4–6 SERVINGS

2 lb. spinach
3 tablespoons olive oil
1 small onion
salt and pepper

3 teaspoons tomato
   purée
hot water
4 oz. Patna rice

Wash the spinach well and chop coarsely. Heat the olive
oil in a saucepan and lightly fry the chopped onion. Toss
in the spinach and sauté for 5–6 minutes. Dilute the
tomato purée in $\frac{1}{4}$ pint hot water, add to the pan and
season to taste. Cover with a lid and simmer gently for
30 minutes. Add about $\frac{1}{2}$ pint hot water and bring to

the boil. Throw in the rice, stir well with a fork and cook gently for a further 15–20 minutes. Remove from the heat, place a napkin on the pan and cover with the lid. Leave in a warm place for 15 minutes before serving.

Spanaki soufflé

Spinach soufflé

8 SERVINGS

2½ oz. butter	8 oz. spinach purée
3½ oz. flour	1 tablespoon finely
⅓ pint hot milk	chopped onion
salt and pepper	7 egg yolks
nutmeg to taste	7 egg whites

Heat the butter in a small saucepan and add the flour. Stir until well blended and the mixture begins to froth and gradually add the hot milk, stirring continuously. Cook gently for 5–10 minutes, season and remove from the heat. Stir in the spinach purée, onion and beaten egg yolks, and when all the ingredients are well blended fold in the stiffly beaten egg whites. Butter a fireproof dish or a soufflé dish and pour in the mixture. Bake in a moderately hot oven for 30 minutes. Serve immediately.

Tyropita me patates

Cheese and potato tart

6 SERVINGS

Filling:

8 oz. flour
1 teaspoon salt
1 teaspoon baking-powder
4 oz. butter or margarine
water to mix

3 medium-sized potatoes (12 oz.)
3 oz. grated Parmesan cheese
3 oz. kefalotyri or cheddar cheese
salt and pepper
3 eggs

Sift the flour, salt and baking-powder into a bowl and rub in the butter. Gradually add enough water to make a firm dough. Roll out to $\frac{1}{4}$ inch thickness and line a large baking tin. Leave for 30 minutes. In the meantime, cook the potatoes in their skins. Peel and mash well or, better, rub through a sieve. Stir in the grated cheeses, season and bind with the well beaten eggs. Put the mixture in the pastry case and bake in a moderately hot oven for 40 minutes.

Arakas me voutiro

Buttered peas

4 SERVINGS

2 lb. peas
3–4 spring onions
3 oz. butter
4 fresh ripe tomatoes or 1 tablespoon tomato purée diluted with $\frac{1}{4}$ pint water

salt and pepper
2 tablespoons chopped dill

Shell the peas, wash and leave in a colander to drain. Cut the spring onions in small pieces, including most of the green part. Heat the butter in a saucepan and sauté the onions, add the peas and sauté for 3–4 minutes. Press the tomatoes through a strainer (or use diluted tomato purée) and add to the pan. Season well, stir in the dill and enough hot water to partly cover the peas. Cover with a lid and simmer gently until the peas are tender and the sauce is considerably thickened.

Melidzanes katsarolas

Aubergines in tomato sauce

4–6 SERVINGS

4 large aubergines
4 oz. butter
1 chopped onion
3 cloves garlic
4–5 ripe tomatoes or
 1 tablespoon tomato
 purée diluted with
 hot water

salt and pepper
2 tablespoons chopped
 parsley
½ pint hot water

Peel the aubergines and cut into thick slices. Put in a basin of cold salted water and leave for 15 minutes. Drain thoroughly. Heat the butter in a saucepan and lightly fry the aubergines. Add the onion and garlic and fry until golden brown. Rub the tomatoes through a sieve, or dilute the tomato purée in a little hot water, and add to the pan. Season well and mix in the chopped parsley and the hot water. Cover the saucepan and cook very gently for 1 hour.

Bamies laderes

Ladies' fingers

4–6 Servings

1½ lb. ladies' fingers (okra)	1 finely chopped onion
salt and pepper	2 cloves garlic
3–4 oz. vinegar	4–5 peeled, chopped tomatoes
4 oz. olive oil	½ pit hot water

Wash the ladies' fingers and drain well. Carefully trim off the stalks without cutting into the flesh and put them in a basin. Sprinkle with salt, pour over the vinegar and leave for 1 hour or so. Heat the olive oil and lightly fry the onion and garlic. Add the peeled and finely chopped tomatoes, season to taste and pour in ½ pint hot water. Cover the pan and simmer for 5–6 minutes. Drain the ladies' fingers and add to the pan. With the lid on cook over low heat for 40–45 minutes, or until tender.

Note:

You can substitute butter for oil, and canned instead of fresh ladies' fingers.

Spanakopitta me avga

Egg and spinach tart

6 Servings

Pastry:

8 oz. flour
1 teaspoon salt
1 teaspoon baking-powder
4 oz. butter
cold water to mix

Filling:

2 lb. spinach
6 tablespoons melted butter
2 egg yolks
2 hard-boiled eggs
salt and pepper
6 oz. chopped ham

Sift the flour, salt and baking-powder and rub in the butter. Gradually add enough water to form a stiff dough. Roll out and line a deep oven dish. Leave for 30 minutes in a cold place. Wash the spinach in several changes of water and plunge in boiling water for 5 minutes. Drain well, pressing out all moisture, and chop finely. Mix in half the melted butter, the lightly beaten egg yolks and seasoning. Arrange the chopped ham in the pastry case, top this with slices of hard-boiled eggs and cover with the spinach mixture. Pour the rest of the butter on top and bake in a moderate oven for 30–35 minutes. Cut in wedges and serve hot.

Kremidopita

Onion pie

6–8 SERVINGS

1 lb. spring onions	6 oz. grated cheese
4 oz. butter	2 tablespoons chopped
salt and pepper	dill
2 tablespoons toasted	4 eggs
breadcrumbs	12 oz. phyllo pastry

Wash and chop the onions, including the green part. Melt 2 oz. butter and toss in the onions. Add a good pinch of salt and pepper and cook gently for 5 minutes. Remove the pan from the heat and mix in the toasted breadcrumbs, cheese and dill. Lightly beat the eggs and stir into the mixture. Melt the rest of the butter and grease a baking tin the size of the pastry (roughly 16 × 12 inches). Line the tin with one sheet of pastry and brush this with the melted butter. Continue in this way until you have used half the quantity of the pastry. Pour in the onion mixture and spread evenly. Cover with the rest of the pastry, brushing each sheet with butter. With a sharp knife score through the top layers to make serving portions. Bake in a moderate oven for 45 minutes.

Pseftikos mousakas

Mock moussaka

6–8 SERVINGS

6 large aubergines	pinch thyme
oil for frying	salt and pepper
2 large onions	5 oz. gruyère cheese
1 oz. butter	4–5 hard-boiled eggs
2 lb. ripe tomatoes	

Slice the aubergines about $\frac{1}{4}$ inch thick, salt them and leave aside for 30–40 minutes, preferably under a plate, to drain away a lot of the water that this vegetable contains. When ready, rinse and dry them and fry in smoking hot olive oil, until crisp and brown. In the meantime, lightly fry the chopped onions in a mixture of oil and butter. Scald the tomatoes and rub through a sieve. Add them to the onions in the pan, also the thyme, salt and pepper, and let the mixture simmer until reduced to a rich, thick pulp. Slice half the cheese and grate the rest.

Spoon half of the sauce into a deep fireproof dish, add a layer of fried aubergines, then a few slices of the cheese and slices of the hard-boiled eggs. Cover with sauce and continue likewise until all the ingredients are used up. The last layer must be of sauce. Sprinkle the grated cheese on top and a few raspings of butter here and there and bake in a hot oven for 15–20 minutes.

Anginares laderes

Artichokes cooked in oil

6–12 SERVINGS

12 medium-sized
  artichokes
juice 2 lemons
½ pint olive oil
1 large chopped onion
1 tablespoon flour

12 shallots or pickling
  onions
1–2 tablespoons chopped
  dill
salt and pepper

Choose young artichokes and remove the outside leaves.
Cut the stalk to within 1 inch of the globe and cut off
about ½ inch from the tips of the inside leaves. If there
is any fuzz (choke) in the middle, remove this with the
point of a sharp knife. Rub each artichoke with half
a cut lemon and drop in a basin of salted water. Put
the olive oil in a skillet and lightly fry the chopped
onion, without letting it colour. Add the flour and stir
until well blended. Drain the artichokes and place on
the onion with sufficient water to cover them completely.
Add the shallots, dill, salt, pepper and lemon juice, and
place a circle of greaseproof paper on top of the artichokes.
Cover the pan with a lid and cook very gently for about
1 hour. Remove from the heat and leave the artichokes
to get cold in the liquid before lifting them on to a serving
dish, stalk side uppermost, and surrounded with the
shallots. Some cooks add small new potatoes to cook
with the artichokes, and sometimes sliced carrots.

Note:

Artichokes are supposed to have many health-giving
properties and in Greece they are recommended to those
with liver or kidney complaints. In such a case, of course,
they are cooked only in lightly salted water and served
with a squeeze of lemon juice.

Anginares me rizi

Artichokes with rice

3–6 SERVINGS

6 large globe artichokes
1 lemon
¼ pint olive oil
4 spring onions
2 tablespoons chopped
dill

salt and pepper
1 pint water
8 oz. Patna rice

Remove the outside coarse leaves from the artichokes
and cut to within 1 inch of the globe. Cut off about ½ inch
from the tips of the rest of the leaves and divide each
artichoke in two. Rub well with ½ lemon and drop
in a bowl of salted water. In the meantime heat the olive
oil in a saucepan and sauté the sliced spring onions
and the dill for 1–2 minutes. Drain the artichoke halves,
place in the pan and cover with the water. Add salt,
pepper and the juice of ½ lemon, cover with a lid and
boil for 5 minutes. Toss in the rice, lower the heat and
simmer covered for 30–40 minutes.

Anginares yemistes

Stuffed artichokes

8 SERVINGS

8 globe artichokes
1 teaspoon lemon juice
2–3 oz. butter
2 chopped onions
12 oz. minced pork
¼ pint wine
¼ pint water
1 tablespoon tomato
purée
1 tablespoon chopped
dill

1 tablespoon chopped
parsley
salt and pepper
1 tablespoon grated
cheese
2 tablespoons
breadcrumbs
½ pint white sauce
(see page 195)

Choose large artichokes. Remove the coarse outside leaves and snip the tips of the other leaves. Cut off the stem to within 1 inch of the globe and remove the choke. Put them in a pan with salted water to cover, add the lemon juice and cook gently for 30 minutes. Do not over-cook, as they must be firm enough to take the stuffing. Remove with a perforated spoon and turn upside down on to a napkin to drain. In the meantime, melt the butter in a saucepan and fry the onion and mince until well browned. Pour in the wine and the water in which you have previously diluted the tomato purée, add the chopped dill and parsley and season to taste. Cook gently until the meat is tender and all the liquid absorbed. Remove from the heat, cool slightly and add the grated cheese and the breadcrumbs. Place the artichokes close together in a shallow baking dish and stuff with the mixture. Cover the tops with the béchamel sauce and cook for 30 minutes in a moderate oven until the tops are golden brown.

Anginares me koukia

Artichokes with broad beans

4 globe artichokes	juice 1 lemon
1½ lb. broad beans	2 tablespoons chopped
¼ pint olive oil	dill
4 spring onions	salt and pepper
½ pint hot water	

Prepare the artichokes as for Artichokes in Oil (see page 171). Shell the broad beans, wash and drain. Heat the olive oil and lightly fry the sliced spring onions. Gradually add the hot water and the lemon juice. Bring to the boil and add the artichokes, beans, dill, salt and pepper. Cover the pan with a lid and cook gently until the vegetables are tender, about 30–35 minutes. This dish can be served hot or cold.

Anginares tiganites (1)

Fried artichokes

8 SERVINGS

8 small globe artichokes
salt and pepper
1 teaspoon lemon juice
4 oz. flour

1 tablespoon olive oil
¼ pint water
2 egg whites
oil for deep frying

Cut off the stalks from the artichokes and remove the coarse outer leaves. Put them into a pan with sufficient water to cover, add seasoning and lemon juice and boil for 15–20 minutes. Remove artichokes with a perforated spoon and drain thoroughly on a napkin. Sift the flour with a pinch of salt and add gradually the olive oil and the water. Mix thoroughly until the batter is quite smooth. Fold in the stiffly-beaten egg whites. Cut the artichoke in halves, or thick slices if preferred, remove the choke and dip into the batter. Fry in smoking hot oil until golden brown. Drain on kitchen paper and serve at once.

Anginares tiganites (2)

Fried artichokes

8 SERVINGS

8 globe artichokes
1 teaspoon lemon juice
salt and pepper
2 eggs
3 tablespoons grated
  cheese

4 tablespoons
  breadcrumbs
deep oil for frying

Cut off the stalks from the artichokes and remove the coarse outer leaves. Put them into a pan with sufficient water to cover, add seasoning and lemon juice and boil for 15–20 minutes. Remove artichokes with a perforated spoon and drain thoroughly in a napkin. Prepare the artichokes as in the previous recipe. Drain well and cut into thick slices. Beat the eggs lightly, dip in the slices and cover thickly with the cheese. Leave for 1–2 minutes. Dip again in the egg and coat with the breadcrumbs. Deep fry in very hot oil until golden brown.

Anginares pastitsio

Artichoke pie

1 lb. minced chuck steak	2 egg yolks
1 chopped onion	¾ pint thick white
3 teaspoons tomato purée	sauce (see page 195)
¼ pint hot water	2 oz. kefalotyri or
salt and pepper	Parmesan cheese,
6 large globe artichokes	grated
½ lemon	8 oz. phyllo pastry
	4 oz. melted butter

Heat 1 oz. butter or margarine and brown the minced meat and onion. Add the tomato purée, previously diluted in the hot water, season to taste and cook in a covered saucepan until there is no liquid left. Cut off the stalk and outer coarse leaves of the artichokes, trim the tops and rub with lemon juice. Cook in boiling salted water for about 20 minutes. Turn upside down to drain thoroughly and cut into slices. Beat the egg yolks into the béchamel sauce and stir in the cheese. Butter a fireproof dish and line with 8 pastry sheets, brushing each sheet with melted butter. Add half the artichoke slices and cover with some of the sauce. Carefully spread the meat mixture on top, one more layer of artichokes and the rest of the béchamel, and cover with the remaining pastry, brushing each sheet with melted butter. Cut through the top layers into squares (as many portions as you require) and bake in a moderate oven for 40–45 minutes.

Anginares me arni avgolemono

Lamb with artichokes in egg and lemon sauce

4–5 SERVINGS

2 lb. lamb	6 large artichokes
3 tablespoons butter	1 tablespoon dill,
1 chopped onion	chopped
1 dessertspoon flour	6 spring onions, chopped
salt and pepper	2 lemons
hot water	2 egg yolks

Wipe the meat and cut into small pieces. Heat the butter in a saucepan and brown the meat. Add the chopped onion and fry lightly without letting it colour. Stir in the flour and seasoning and when well blended pour in about ½ pint hot water, or enough to cover the meat. Cover the pan and cook slowly for 30 minutes. In the meantime, prepare the artichokes as for Artichoke Pie (see p. 175). Rub with lemon juice and leave in a bowl of salted water. When the meat is partly cooked cut the artichokes in half, drain and add to the pan with the dill and the sliced spring onions (white part only) and the juice of ½ lemon. Cover the pan and simmer until both meat and artichokes are tender and there is only about 6 tablespoons liquid left in the pan. Beat the egg yolks with the juice of 1 lemon in a small basin, remove the pan from the heat and gradually add the liquid into the egg and lemon mixture, beating all the time. Pour the mixture over the meat and artichokes and return the pan to a very low heat until the sauce thickens. Do not let the sauce boil.

Anginares me avga

Artichokes in custard

4 SERVINGS

4 medium-sized
  artichokes
juice ½ lemon

4 tablespoons butter
2 eggs
salt and pepper

Cut off the stalks from the artichokes, remove the coarse
outside leaves, and cut each in two. Drop in a pan of
boiling salted water in which you have previously added
the lemon juice and cook gently for 20–30 minutes. In
the meantime heat the butter in a frying pan, drain the
artichokes, dip in flour and fry lightly. Beat the eggs with
2 tablespoons water and seasoning to taste and pour
over the artichokes. Lower the heat and cook until the
eggs are set. Serve immediately.

Patatokeftedes

Potato cakes

4–6 SERVINGS

2 lb. potatoes
3 eggs
4 oz. grated cheese
salt and pepper

pinch nutmeg
2 tablespoons flour
oil for frying

Scrub the potatoes and put them to boil in lightly salted
cold water. Skin and put through a 'mouli' sieve. When
the potatoes are cold add the eggs one at a time and
mix in the grated cheese and seasoning. Form into small
flat cakes, dip in flour and fry in smoking hot oil until
both sides are golden brown. Drain on kitchen paper
and serve hot or cold.

Rice, Pasta, Egg and Cheese Dishes

Rice cooked the Greek way does not require rinsing, drying and reheating, a rather tedious and long drawn out process, particularly when you are pressed for time. Yet it produces perfectly cooked rice with each grain dry, separate and glistening.

Pasta also takes on a new meaning and there are many unusual ways of cooking it.

A *Pastitsio* of macaroni is a good way of making a little meat go a long way and it can be adapted to suit any occasion, from the mid-week family dinner to the special supper for guests.

Tiganites me rizi

Rice fritters

4-6 SERVINGS

3 eggs
2 level tablespoons flour
12 oz. cooked rice
pinch salt

butter for frying
apricot or other jam
lemon juice

Lightly beat the eggs and fold in the flour, rice and seasoning. Heat the butter in a frying pan and drop spoonfuls of the mixture. Cook until golden brown on both sides. Drain on paper and serve very hot with jam, previously diluted with a little lemon juice.

Pilafi me saltsa domata

Pilaf with tomato sauce

4 SERVINGS

4 oz. butter
1 finely chopped onion
1 crushed clove garlic
5 peeled tomatoes
1 tablespoon finely
  chopped celery

1 tablespoon finely
chopped parsley
salt and pepper
pinch cinnamon
12 oz. Patna rice

Heat 2 oz. butter in a small saucepan and lightly fry the onion and garlic. Add the tomatoes, celery, parsley and seasoning, cover the pan and simmer for 25 minutes. Rub the sauce through a sieve and return to the pan. Keep hot. In the meantime, cook the rice in plenty of boiling salted water until tender. Strain and rinse. Return to the pan over gentle heat. Melt the rest of the butter and when smoking hot pour over the rice, stir lightly with a fork and pack into a mould or basin. Turn on to a serving dish and top with the sauce, which should be thick and rich.

Krokettes rizi

Rice croquettes

4 SERVINGS

½ pint water
4 oz. rice
½ oz. butter
salt and pepper
3 tablespoons grated
cheese
2 tablespoons finely
chopped ham

pinch nutmeg
flour
1 egg
toasted breadcrumbs
fat for frying

Put the water in a saucepan, add the butter and seasoning and bring to the boil. Throw in the rice, stir well and cover the pan with a lid. Simmer gently until there is no liquid left and the rice is tender. Remove from the heat and stir in the cheese, ham and a good pinch of nutmeg. Mix thoroughly. Take one tablespoonful of the mixture, roll it in flour and shape into a sausage or a small ball. Dip in egg and crumbs and fry quickly in smoking hot fat until golden brown.

Rizi pilafi

Rice pilaf

4–6 SERVINGS

2 pints meat or chicken
stock
2 oz. butter

1 lb. long grain rice
salt and pepper

Bring the stock to the boil, add half the butter and season well. Add the rice, previously washed and drained, and stir well with a fork. After 5–6 minutes steady boiling turn down the heat, cover the pan and simmer gently for 15 minutes, when all the stock should be absorbed and the rice tender. Remove from the heat and uncover.

Put a napkin or a piece of flannel on top of the saucepan, cover with the lid and put at the back of the stove for 15–20 minutes for the rice to 'steam'. Melt the rest of the butter and pour over the rice. Stir lightly with a fork to separate the grains and serve at once.

Pilafi me astako

Lobster pilaf

4–6 SERVINGS

1 medium-sized lobster cooked
2 tablespoons olive oil
2 tablespoons butter
2 onions grated
1 teaspoon sugar
4 tomatoes, skinned and sliced
2 teaspoons chopped parsley
salt and pepper
4 tablespoons dry white wine
¼ pint water

For pilaf:

1 lb. long grain rice
2 pints meat or chicken stock
1 oz. butter
salt and pepper

Heat the oil and butter in a saucepan and add the onions. Fry until golden brown, sprinkle with the sugar and add the tomatoes, parsley and seasoning. Simmer gently for a few minutes, pour in the wine and water and mix well. Cover and cook over gentle heat for about 30 minutes, until the contents are reduced to a thick sauce. Cut the lobster meat into small pieces and drop in the sauce. Let it simmer for a further 5–10 minutes.

If fresh lobster is not available, a can of suitable size may be used instead.

Make the pilaf as for Rice Pilaf (see p. 180). Put in a ring mould and press down well. Turn out and pour the lobster sauce in the middle.

Pilafi gratine

Pilaf au gratin

4 SERVINGS

2 pints stock
salt
1 lb. long grain rice
4 oz. ham or smoked
tongue
2½ oz. butter
4 tablespoons flour
¾ pint milk

nutmeg
salt and pepper
2 tablespoons grated
cheese
2 tablespoons
breadcrumbs

Bring the stock to boil and add 1 oz. of the butter and salt. Throw in the rice and boil for 5–7 minutes. Lower the heat, cover and simmer gently until the rice is tender and there is no liquid left. Chop the ham or tongue in very small pieces and mix well with the rice. Keep warm. Melt the rest of the butter in a saucepan over gentle heat. Add the flour and stir until it begins to honeycomb, but do not let it colour. Add the warm milk gradually, stir and let it simmer gently until the sauce thickens. Season to taste and add the grated nutmeg. Grease a fireproof dish and spread a thin layer of the sauce. Empty the rice on top and cover with the rest of the sauce. Sprinkle with grated cheese and breadcrumbs and dot with a few shavings of butter. Place in a moderate oven for about 30 minutes, or until the top is golden brown.

Note:

Left-over rice can be used for this recipe. Just warm up before adding the ham and proceed as above.

Midia pilafi

Pilaf with mussels

4–6 SERVINGS

1 quart mussels in their
  shells
6 tablespoons olive oil
2 medium-sized onions
1¾ pints water

¼ pint dry white wine
2–3 tomatoes, skinned
  and chopped
salt and pepper
1 lb. Patna rice

Scrape the mussels with a knife and wash thoroughly.
Heat the oil in a large saucepan, add the chopped onions
and fry until pale brown. Add the mussels, cover the
saucepan and cook over gentle heat until all the shells
are open. Pour in the water and the wine and add the
tomatoes. Season well. Bring once to the boil, reduce
the heat and cook gently for 10 minutes. Remove the
mussels from the sauce, open completely and pick out
the flesh. Return this to the pan and add the rice.
Continue cooking over low heat for a further 15–20
minutes, or until the rice is tender. Remove pan to
the back of the stove, put a napkin under the lid and
let the rice rest for 20 minutes. Fluff the rice up with
a fork and serve at once.

Pilafi me kima

Pilaf with minced meat

4 Servings

4 oz. butter
10 oz. rice
4 tablespoons olive oil
1 lb. minced steak
1 finely chopped onion
1 clove garlic, crushed
pinch sugar

salt and pepper
4–5 peeled and chopped
  tomatoes
1–2 tablespoons water
1 pint boiling water
4 oz. grated Parmesan
  cheese

Heat the butter and fry the rice until just beginning to
colour. Heat the oil in a large saucepan and lightly fry
the meat and onion. Add the crushed garlic, sugar,
seasoning and tomatoes and 1–2 tablespoons water, and
simmer for about 30 minutes. Pour in about 1 pint
boiling water and add the fried rice. Cover the pan
with a lid and cook over low heat for 18 minutes. Remove
from the heat, stir in the cheese and adjust the seasoning.
Serve really hot.

Rizi soufflé

Rice soufflé

4 Servings

1½ oz. butter
4 tablespoons flour
⅓ pint milk (scant)
4 tablespoons cooked rice

8 oz. grated cheese
salt and pepper
4 eggs, separated

Heat the butter in a small saucepan, add the flour and
cook over low heat for 1–2 minutes. Pour in the milk
gradually and cook for a further 5 minutes, or until the
thickens, stirring all the while. Remove from the
add the rice, grated cheese, seasoning and

lightly beaten egg yolks. When all these ingredients are thoroughly blended fold in the stiffly beaten egg whites. Turn the mixture into a greased soufflé dish and bake in a moderate oven for 30–35 minutes. Serve immediately.

Manitaria me rizi

Mushrooms with rice

4 SERVINGS

4 tablespoons olive oil
2 tablespoons finely chopped onion
8 oz. mushrooms
4 tablespoons finely chopped celery
2 tablespoons finely chopped parsley
$\frac{1}{4}$ pint stock
$\frac{1}{4}$ pint dry white wine
salt and pepper
4 oz. rice

Heat the olive oil in a skillet and fry the onion until golden brown. Peel and slice the mushrooms and cook with the onion for a further 2–3 minutes. Mix in the celery, parsley, stock and wine, and season well. Cover the pan with a lid and simmer for 15–20 minutes. Stir in the rice and cook gently for a further 20 minutes, or until the rice is tender and all the liquid in the pan has been absorbed.

Avga me yaourti

Poached eggs with yoghurt

2 SERVINGS

1 jar yoghurt
2 eggs
salt and pepper

1 tablespoon melted
butter

Divide the yoghurt into small individual dishes. Poach the eggs in salted boiling water, in which you have added a few drops of vinegar. Cook until set, without letting the water boil again. Remove eggs with a perforated spoon, trim and place on the yoghurt. Sprinkle with salt and pepper and sprinkle with the melted butter.

Makaronia me avga gratin

Eggs and macaroni au gratin

4 SERVINGS

8 oz. macaroni
2 oz. butter
4 oz. grated cheese
4 hard-boiled eggs
4 level tablespoons flour

½ pint hot milk
salt and pepper
knob butter
3 tablespoons toasted
breadcrumbs

Cook the macaroni in plenty of boiling salted water. Strain, add ¼ of the butter and ½ the cheese and mix thoroughly. Butter a pie dish, put in the macaroni and arrange the egg slices on top. Heat the remaining butter, stir in the flour and cook over low heat for 1–2 minutes. Add the hot milk gradually and season to taste. Cook for 5 minutes, stirring continuously, and pour the sauce over the macaroni dish. Sprinkle with crumbs, the rest of the cheese and the knob of butter cut into tiny pieces. Cook in a moderate oven for 20–25 minutes, or until nicely golden on top.

Pastitsio makaroni me yemissi

Macaroni pie with meat filling

4–6 SERVINGS

4 oz. butter
1 lb. sausage meat
1 large chopped onion
2 tablespoons tomato
    purée
little hot water
¼ pint wine
1 tablespoon chopped
    parsley

salt and pepper
1 lb. macaroni
2 oz. grated cheese
1 teaspoon cornflour
¼ pint milk
2 egg yolks

Heat 2 oz. of the butter in a saucepan and fry the sausage meat with the onion. Dilute the purée in a little hot water and add to the sausage meat together with the wine, chopped parsley and seasoning. Cover and cook gently for 30 minutes. Cook the macaroni in salted, boiling water for 15–20 minutes. Drain and mix with the rest of the butter and the grated cheese. Grease a pie dish and put in half the macaroni, cover with the meat filling and top with the rest of the macaroni. Dilute the cornflour in the milk and beat in the 2 egg yolks. Pour over the dish and cook in a moderate oven for 25–30 minutes, or until golden brown.

Pastitsio makaronia

Macaroni cheese

4–6 SERVINGS

1 lb. macaroni
4 oz. butter
4 oz. grated cheese
½ pint white sauce
(see page 195)

1 egg yolk
salt and pepper
nutmeg
2 tablespoons toasted
breadcrumbs

Cook the macaroni in a large saucepan of salted boiling water for about 20 minutes. Do not over-cook. Drain, return to the pan and stir in 3 oz. butter and 3 oz. cheese. Cover and leave for 2–3 minutes. In the meantime prepare the béchamel sauce and beat in the egg yolk and a good pinch of nutmeg. Grease a pie dish and sprinkle with one tablespoon of toasted breadcrumbs. Put in the macaroni and cover with the sauce. Sprinkle the top with the rest of the cheese, crumbs and butter cut into very small pieces. Bake in a moderate oven for 15–20 minutes, or until golden brown.

Nokky

Gnocchi

4 SERVINGS

1 lb. cooked potatoes,
mashed
2 eggs
1½ oz. butter
6 oz. flour
4 oz. grated cheese

2 tablespoons olive oil
1 onion
1 clove garlic
1 lb. tomatoes
chopped parsley
salt and pepper

Put the mashed potatoes in a bowl, add the eggs, half the butter and the flour. Blend the mixture thoroughly, shape into tiny balls — the size of a hazel-nut — and drop into a pan of boiling salted water. When the balls float to the surface, they are cooked. Drain with a perforated spoon, place on a dish and cover thickly with the grated cheese. In the meantime heat the olive oil and lightly fry the chopped onion and garlic. Add the peeled and finely chopped tomatoes, the parsley and seasoning. Simmer gently for 20–25 minutes. Pour the sauce over the gnocchi and serve immediately.

Omeletta me loukanika

Omelette with frankfurters

6 SERVINGS

4 frankfurters	8 eggs
2 oz. butter	4 teaspoons water
1 medium-sized onion	salt and pepper

Plunge the frankfurters into hot water for 5 minutes. Remove and slice about $\frac{1}{4}$ inch thick. Melt the butter in an omelette pan and fry the finely chopped onion until it begins to colour. Add the sausage slices, mix thoroughly and continue to fry until the onion is golden brown. Beat the eggs very lightly with a fork, add the water and seasoning and pour into the frying pan. When the underneath is set, lift the sides with a fork and let the uncooked part run under. While still moist on top fold over and slide on to a warm dish. Serve at once.

Omeletta me renga

Kipper omelette

4 SERVINGS

2 kippers
2 tablespoons olive oil
6 eggs

salt and pepper
1 tablespoon chopped
parsley

Bone the kippers and cut flesh into small dice. Put the oil in a frying pan and when really hot add the kippers and fry for 3–4 minutes. In the meantime beat the eggs lightly, add salt, pepper and chopped parsley and pour into the pan. Stir once or twice, and when the omelette is beginning to set lift the sides and let the uncooked portion roll under. When ready, fold over and slide on to a warm dish. Sprinkle some parsley on top and serve at once.

Kolokithia omeletta

Courgette omelette

4–6 SERVINGS

1½ lb. courgettes,
or marrow
1 slice toasted bread
4–5 tablespoons milk
6 tablespoons olive oil ·
1 small chopped onion

2 tomatoes, peeled
and chopped
salt and pepper
4–5 eggs
2 tablespoons grated
Parmesan cheese

Scrape the courgettes lightly and cut into small rounds, or peel and dice the marrow, removing the seeds. Put the toast to soak in the milk. Heat the olive oil in a frying pan and sauté the onion and courgettes for 5–6 minutes. Add the tomatoes and seasoning, cover and cook gently for a further 10 minutes. Beat the eggs, add the cheese and the soaked and mashed toast, and pour over the courgettes in the pan. Stir lightly with a wooden spoon and when the omelette is done on one side turn over and return to the pan to cook the underside. Serve flat and cut into wedges.

Omeletta me rizi

Rice omelette

4–6 SERVINGS

3–4 medium-sized tomatoes
toasted breadcrumbs
little sugar
flour
butter for frying
5–6 eggs
5–6 tablespoons milk
salt and pepper
6–7 tablespoons cooked rice
1 tablespoon chopped onion
parsley

Cut the tomatoes in thick slices. Mix the breadcrumbs, sugar and seasoning and well cover the tomato slices. Dip in flour and fry in a little butter. Remove to a dish and keep hot. Beat the eggs with the milk, salt and pepper and mix in the cooked rice. Fry the onions and when golden brown pour in the egg mixture, stir well with a fork to distribute the rice and onions evenly and cook the omelette as usual. Turn on to a serving dish and sprinkle the chopped parsley on top. Place the tomato slices round the omelette and serve immediately.

Omeletta me kima

Minced meat omelette

2–3 SERVINGS

3 tablespoons best
quality minced steak
1 finely chopped onion
salt and pepper
1 oz. butter
2 tomatoes, finely
chopped

2–3 tablespoons hot
water
4 eggs
2 tablespoons milk
1 tablespoon grated
cheese

Put the minced meat and onion in a small saucepan,
add a good pinch of pepper and cook over gentle heat,
until the mince looks dry. Add half the butter and fry
until nicely brown. Season with salt and mix in the
skinned and finely chopped tomatoes and 2–3 tablespoons
hot water. Continue to cook gently until there is no liquid
left and the meat is tender. Beat the eggs lightly and
gradually add the milk, cheese and seasoning. Melt the
rest of the butter in an omelette pan and when hot pour
in the eggs. When the omelette is ready, remove from
the heat, put the meat in the middle lengthwise and
roll up. Slide on to a warm dish and serve at once.

Omeletta me solomo

Salmon omelette

2–3 SERVINGS

1 small can salmon
4 eggs, separated
4 tablespoons olive oil

1 tablespoon finely
chopped parsley
salt and pepper

Remove the skin and bones from salmon and chop very
finely. Beat the egg yolks lightly, add 2 tablespoons
of olive oil and the parsley and season to taste. Pour

in a small saucepan and stir over gentle heat until all the ingredients are well blended, but do not allow the mixture to boil. Remove from the heat and mix in the salmon. When the mixture is cold fold in the stiffly beaten egg whites. Heat the rest of the oil in an omelette pan, pour in the eggs and cook as for plain omelette.

Tyropita

Cheese tart

4 SERVINGS

12 oz. feta or white Cheshire cheese
½ pint white sauce (see page 195)
3 eggs

salt and white pepper
nutmeg
½ lb. phyllo pastry
4–5 oz. melted butter

Rinse the feta in cold water and mash well, or grate the Cheshire cheese. Make the sauce and when cool beat in the eggs and add the cheese, salt and pepper and nutmeg. Grease a rectangular baking tin slightly smaller than the pastry and line with one pastry sheet. Brush this with melted butter and add a second sheet, continuing in this way until you have used half the quantity of the pastry. Pour in the filling and turn up the overhanging pastry to enclose the filling round the edges. Cover with the remaining pastry, brushing each sheet with melted butter. Turn the top sheets under and pour the rest of the butter on top, spreading it evenly. With the point of a sharp knife cut into squares or diamonds. Do not drag the knife. Bake in a moderate oven for 30 minutes, or until the surface is golden. Eat hot or cold.

Sauces

The basic Greek sauces are not numerous, but there are many variations on the same theme with the result that each sauce can be adapted to fish, flesh, fowl and vegetable. The classical *avgolemono* is the national sauce, which is simple, easy to prepare, and delicious to eat. It is followed closely in popularity by the *skordalia* for the garlic lovers. Rosemary sauce for fried fish or liver, and the plain olive oil, lemon, parsley or dill dressing for salads and grilled fish, are both quick and appetising.

Avgolemono

Egg and lemon sauce

4 SERVINGS

2 egg yolks
2 tablespoons lemon juice

3–4 tablespoons hot liquid

Beat the egg yolks with the lemon juice and very gradually add the hot liquid. This can be chicken broth, fish stock or vegetable stock according to the dish in which you are going to use the sauce. Beat continuously and return to the stock pan, which you have previously removed from the heat. Stir well and do not let boil once the eggs have been added.

Saltsa crema

Greek white sauce

6–8 SERVINGS

4–5 oz. butter
2 tablespoons flour
½ pint hot milk

salt and pepper
2 egg yolks
1 teaspoon lemon juice

Melt 1 oz. of the butter in a small saucepan and add the flour. Stir over low heat for 2–3 minutes and gradually add the hot milk. Season to taste and beat in the egg yolks. Stir in the rest of the butter cut up in small pieces and finally add the lemon juice.

Mayonneza

Mayonnaise sauce

4 SERVINGS

2 egg yolks
½ teaspoon salt
pinch white pepper
1 teaspoon mustard

pinch sugar
½ pint olive oil
2 tablespoons lemon juice
  or wine vinegar

Mix the egg yolks, salt, pepper, mustard and sugar in a small bowl and when thoroughly blended add the oil drop by drop, beating all the time with a wire whisk. After a quarter of the oil has been added increase the flow gradually and add a few teaspoons of vinegar or lemon juice. Whisk and continue to add the oil and vinegar until all the ingredients have been used up.

For a pouring mayonnaise add 2 tablespoons cream or wine and mix thoroughly.

For a light foamy mayonnaise fold in a stiffly beaten egg white. For a stiff mayonnaise to cover fish, eggs or chicken, or to use as garnish, soak 2 sheets gelatine in a little cold water and dissolve over boiling water. When cold, but not set, stir into the mayonnaise sauce and mix thoroughly.

Mayonneza tis stigmis

Quick mayonnaise

4 SERVINGS

7 level tablespoons
cornflour
¼ pint water
¼ pint milk
2 egg yolks
1 teaspoon salt
½ teaspoon white pepper

2 teaspoons mustard
2 teaspoons wine
vinegar
⅛ pint olive oil
2–3 tablespoons lemon
juice

Blend the cornflour with ⅛ pint of water. Put the rest of the water and milk in a small saucepan and bring to the boil. Add the blended cornflour and stir until the mixture is smooth and creamy. Pour this into a bowl and allow to cool. Mix the yolks with the salt, pepper, mustard and vinegar, and beat with a wire whisk until well blended. Add the egg mixture to the cornflour and gradually beat in the olive oil, alternating with the lemon juice. Beat thoroughly and keep in a cold place or a refrigerator to be used as required.

Note:

This mayonnaise sauce may not appeal to the purists, but it has the advantage of being economical, easy and quick.

Skordalia mayonaisa

Garlic mayonnaise

5 cloves garlic
1 teaspoon salt
4 oz. ground almonds
1 medium-sized potato,
cooked

1 tablespoon water
1 egg yolk
½ pint olive oil
1–2 tablespoons wine
vinegar

Put the garlic and salt in a mortar and pound until very smooth. Add the ground almonds and continue pounding. Mash the potato and add to the garlic mixture and stir in the water. When all the ingredients are thoroughly blended, transfer the mixture to a basin and mix in the egg yolk. Add the oil drop by drop at first and beating all the while with a wire whisk. Gradually add a little vinegar to loosen the mixture, then the rest of the oil in spoonfuls and finally the rest of the vinegar. This mixture should be roughly the consistency of mayonnaise and it can be served with courgette or aubergine fritters, French fried potatoes, beetroot or fried mussels.

Skordalia

Garlic sauce

4–5 cloves of garlic	2–3 tablespoons vinegar
1 teaspoon salt	2 thick slices bread
6 oz. shelled walnuts	1–2 tablespoons water
¼ pint olive oil	

Pound the garlic with the salt and the walnuts until well blended and creamy. Soak the bread in water, squeeze dry and add to the other ingredients. Mix thoroughly and add gradually the oil and vinegar. Finally add the water. Use as suggested in the previous recipe.

Ladoxitho

Oil and vinegar dressing

6 SERVINGS

6 tablespoons best olive
  oil
4 tablespoons wine
  vinegar
2 tablespoons water
1 tablespoon finely
  chopped parsley
salt and pepper

Put all the ingredients together in a basin and whisk until thoroughly blended. Use as required.

Saltsa domata

Tomato sauce

6–8 SERVINGS

1½ tablespoons butter
1 tablespoon chopped
  onion
1 tablespoon chopped
  carrot
1 tablespoon chopped
  celery
1 tablespoon chopped
  parsley
1 crushed clove garlic
1 level tablespoon
  flour
1½ lb. fresh tomatoes
½ pint stock or water
salt and pepper
1 bay leaf
1 teaspoon sugar

Heat the butter and lightly fry the onion. Add the carrot, celery, parsley and garlic, and fry for 3–4 minutes. Stir in the flour and mix well. Skin and chop the tomatoes and add to the contents of the pan. Add stock, season well and add the bay leaf and the sugar. Bring to the boil and lower the heat to simmer the sauce for 25–30 minutes. Press through a sieve or a strainer and use as required. If the sauce is too thick add 1–2 tablespoons water and boil for 1 minute more.

Desserts, Cakes and Pastries

In spite of the fact that the average Greek prefers to finish off his meal with fresh fruit — of which there is an abundance all the year round — he still manages to consume a vast amount of sweet stuff: perhaps too sweet at times for non-Greek tastes.

In the middle of the morning, the afternoon, the evening, in fact at any time of the day, you will see them sitting at open air cafés or pastry shops eating luscious cakes and pastries accompanied by the inevitable glass of iced water. There is a different kind of cake or pastry for practically every festive occasion, and as there are many such occasions in the Greek calendar the variety is naturally imposing! Some of the cakes are not unlike English cakes, but most of them are of the gâteau variety. The pastries, on the other hand, are quite different, but not difficult to make at home, if you can buy *phyllo* or *kataifi* pastry.

As in ancient Greece, the favourite ingredients are honey and nuts of all kinds, and nowadays brandy, spices and chocolate add to the variety. Chestnuts are very popular, and a sweetened, vanilla-flavoured chestnut purée topped with ice-cream is one of the easiest desserts to prepare.

Yaourti

Yoghurt (1)

An American dietician advises: 'If you want to look younger and live longer, eat one pint of yoghurt a day.' In Greece and the other Balkan countries, where yoghurt forms part of the diet, many other virtues are claimed for it, such as a cure for a hangover, stomach troubles, sunburn and many more. Yoghurt is produced commercially by the addition of a bacterial culture, the *Bacillus bulgaricus* to fresh milk. It can be made at home quite easily and cheaply by using commercially prepared yoghurt to start your own culture. In Greece it is made with sheep's milk, which has a higher fat content than other types of milk, and often it is thick enough to cut with a knife. In Britain, cow's and sometimes goat's milk is widely used, and sometimes it is specially fortified.

2–3 SERVINGS

1 pint best milk   1 good teaspoon yoghurt

Bring the milk to the boil and pour into a bowl. Allow to cool to blood heat. Dilute the culture in a little tepid milk and add it to the bowl, trying not to disturb the skin on top of the milk more than necessary. Place the bowl in a warm place or in a pan of gently simmering water, cover with a thick cloth and leave until thick. Remove to a cold place or a refrigerator.

Yaourti

Yoghourt (2)

4 Servings

2 pints milk
3 tablespoons prepared yoghurt

3 oz. skimmed milk powder

Add the milk powder to the fresh milk, mix thoroughly and heat until lukewarm. Stir in the prepared yoghurt and empty into a bowl. Place the bowl in a pan containing hot water, cover with a thick cloth to keep it warm and leave for about 5 hours. The water in the pan should be between 105° and 120° until the yoghurt sets. Serve very cold.

Froutosalata me yaourti

Fruit salad with yoghurt

4 Servings

2 bananas
2 oranges
1 apple

2 tablespoons brandy
8 oz. yoghurt
4 oz. castor sugar

Peel the bananas, oranges and apple and cut into small pieces. Stir in the brandy and mix well. Leave in a cool place for at least one hour. Beat the yoghurt with the sugar and mix lightly into the fruit. Chill and serve immediately.

Halvas simigdalenios

Semolina halva

6 SERVINGS

4 oz. butter
6 oz. coarse semolina
2 tablespoons blanched
  almonds or pine kernels
10 oz. sugar
¼ pint milk

½ pint water
1-inch stick cinnamon
3 cloves
lemon peel
1 tablespoon ground
  cinnamon

Heat the butter in a thick-bottomed saucepan and when sizzling add the semolina and the pine kernels, or blanched almonds, cut in slivers. Cook over gentle heat, stirring continuously with a wooden spoon until the semolina begins to colour. In the meantime, put the sugar, milk, water, the cinnamon stick, cloves and lemon peel in a small saucepan and boil for 2–3 minutes. Remove the cinnamon, cloves and peel, and pour the boiling syrup over the semolina. Stir over gentle heat until the mixture thickens. Remove from the heat, cover with a napkin and put the lid on the pan. Leave in a warm place for 5–10 minutes. Pack in a mould and turn on to a serving dish, or use an ice-cream scoop. Sprinkle with cinnamon and serve.

Krema tiganiti

Custard fritters

4–6 SERVINGS

1 oz. flour
1 oz. cornflour
3 oz. sugar
1¼ pint milk
3 eggs
1 egg yolk

4–5 tablespoons sifted
  biscuit crumbs or
  toasted breadcrumbs
fat for frying
vanilla sugar

Mix the flour, cornflour and sugar with a little of the cold milk. Boil the rest of the milk and pour into the mixture, stirring well. Return to the pan and cook gently for 5 minutes. Add the 3 beaten eggs and cook for a few minutes longer without boiling. Pour the custard into a buttered shallow tray and spread evenly to a depth of 1 inch. When quite cold cut into squares or oblongs, using a sharp, floured knife, dip in the lightly beaten egg yolk and cover with the crumbs. Fry in very hot fat, a few at a time, until golden brown. Drain, sprinkle with vanilla sugar and serve immediately.

Moustalevria

Grape juice and semolina mould

4 SERVINGS

1½ pints grape juice	1 tablespoon sesame
4½ tablespoons fine	seeds
semolina	cinnamon
4 oz. grated walnuts	sugar (optional)

Bring the grape juice to the boil and stir in the semolina. Cook over low heat, stirring continuously, until the mixture is thick and big bubbles appear on the surface. Pour into individual glasses. When cold and set, sprinkle with nuts, sesame seeds and cinnamon to taste. If the grape juice is not sweet enough, add some sugar or honey while cooking.

Note:

In Greece the grape juice is first cleared by the addition of a small quantity of wood ashes tied in a muslin bag. It is then brought to the boil, skimmed, strained and used in various ways. In other countries it is sold in bottles or cans, already free of sediment.

Rizogalo

Creamed rice

4 SERVINGS

1 pint milk	4 oz. sugar
strip lemon peel	2 egg yolks
5 tablespoons rice	1 tablespoon milk

Put the milk and lemon peel in a saucepan and bring slowly to the boil. Sprinkle in the rice, stirring well to prevent it from going lumpy, and when partly cooked add the sugar. Simmer gently until the rice is tender and the mixture creamy. Remove the pan from the heat. Beat the 2 egg yolks with the 1 tablespoon milk and stir into the rice. Return to the heat, and just before it reaches boiling point remove again and pour into individual glass dishes. Serve ice cold.

Mila yemista marenga

Stuffed apples with meringue

4 SERVINGS

6 oz. sugar	4 tablespoons icing sugar
little water	1 tablespoon flour
$\frac{1}{2}$ lemon	$\frac{1}{4}$ pint milk
4 medium-sized apples	1 egg white
1 egg yolk	

In a small saucepan prepare a syrup with the 6 oz. sugar, a little water and a squeeze of lemon juice. Simmer gently for 10 minutes. Peel the apples, but leave whole. Plunge them in the syrup and see that they are completely covered. Simmer for 5–6 minutes. Drain well, slice off the top and remove the core with a small spoon. Leave aside. Beat the egg yolk with 2 tablespoons icing sugar, add the grated rind of the lemon and mix in the flour very carefully, so as not to make it lumpy. Warm the milk and gradually add to the egg mixture. Return to the pan and boil up once. Remove from the heat and cool. Place the apples on a greased tin and fill with the mixture. Whip the egg white until stiff and fold in the rest of the icing sugar. Put a spoonful on each apple and bake in a moderate oven for 30 minutes.

Avgokalamara

Sweet fritters

8 SERVINGS

1½ lb. semolina	*Syrup:*
pinch salt	honey
4–5 eggs	little water
2 oranges	ground walnuts
cold water	ground cinnamon
deep oil for frying	icing sugar

Put the semolina in a basin and add the salt, the eggs one at a time and the juice of the oranges. Mix well, adding enough water to make a stiff dough: if too stiff add a little more water. Roll out thinly and cut into ribbons or any other shape you like. Just before dropping them in smoking hot oil crumble them a little with your hands, or twist them into a knot. Fry until golden brown, drain on kitchen paper and remove to a serving dish. Dilute some honey with warm water and pour over the avgokalamara, sprinkle with the nuts, cinnamon and sifted icing sugar.

Tiganites me stafides

Fritters with dried fruit

8 SERVINGS

6 oz. flour
2 teaspoons baking
  powder
pinch salt
2 oz. sugar
1 oz. currants
1 oz. sultanas

vanilla or lemon essence
1 egg
¼ pint milk and water,
  mixed
deep oil for frying
icing sugar
cinnamon

Sift the flour, baking powder and salt, and add the sugar and dried fruit. Make a well in the middle and stir in the beaten egg mixed with flavouring to taste, and gradually pour in the milk and water mixture. Beat for a few minutes. Drop spoonfuls of the batter in smoking hot oil and fry until golden brown on both sides. Drain on kitchen paper and sprinkle with sugar and cinnamon.

Portokali komposta

Orange compote

4 SERVINGS

4 oranges
8 oz. sugar
¼ pint water

strip orange peel
1 tablespoon Cointreau

Peel the oranges and cut into rounds. Remove pith and pips and place in a glass bowl. Boil the sugar, water and orange peel together until they form a light syrup, add the liqueur and pour over the oranges. Add a few tiny slivers of orange zest and leave the compote to get cold.

Kastana komposta

Chestnut compote

6–8 SERVINGS

1½ lb. large chestnuts
½ pint water
8 oz. sugar

small piece cinnamon
or vanilla pod

Peel the chestnuts and put them to boil for 10 minutes. Remove the inside skin and drain. Put the water, sugar and flavouring in a saucepan, bring to the boil and let it simmer until it forms a light syrup. Throw in the chestnuts, cover the pan and cook slowly until the chestnuts are tender but remain whole. Serve cold.

Glykisma me myla

Apple pudding

4 SERVINGS

8 oz. stale bread
¾ pint hot milk
2 eggs, separated
3 oz. sugar
½ teaspoon grated
lemon rind

1 teaspoon cinnamon
4 eating apples
2 tablespoons melted
butter
2 tablespoons brandy

Remove the crusts and soak the bread in the hot milk. Mash and press through a sieve. Stir in the 2 egg yolks, the sugar, cinnamon and lemon rind. Peel and cut the apples into small dice and add to the mixture. Lastly fold in the stiffly beaten egg whites. Grease and flour a fireproof dish and pour in the pudding mixture. Spoon the melted butter all over the top and bake in a moderate oven for 45 minutes. Pour the brandy over the pudding while still hot. This pudding can be eaten hot or cold.

Rizogalo me myla

Rice and apple pudding

4–5 SERVINGS

1 pint milk
4 oz. sugar
5 tablespoons rice
1 tablespoon cornflour
little cold milk
3 eating apples

extra sugar
3 teaspoons cinnamon
(or to taste)
3 tablespoons toasted
breadcrumbs
knob butter

Bring the milk to the boil with 2 oz. of the sugar and sprinkle in the rice, stirring well with a fork to prevent from going lumpy. Simmer gently until the rice is almost cooked. Dilute the cornflour in a little cold milk, stir in and continue to cook until the rice is tender and the pudding thick and creamy. Peel, core and cut the apples into rounds. Put a layer of rice in a greased oven dish and cover with a layer of apples. Sprinkle with sugar and cinnamon and add a second layer of rice. Finish off with a layer of apple rings. Sprinkle with the remaining sugar, cinnamon and the toasted breadcrumbs; cut the knob of butter into very small dice and dot here and there. Bake in a moderate oven for 15–20 minutes. This pudding may be served hot or cold.

Glykisma mandariniou

Tangerine cake

4 oz. butter
8 oz. castor sugar
3 eggs
rind and juice
2 tangerines

10 oz. self-raising flour
2 oz. sultanas
3 tablespoons brandy
icing sugar

Beat the butter with the sugar until light and fluffy. Add the eggs one at a time and beat well. Stir in the grated rind and juice of the tangerines and fold in the flour. Add the sultanas and finally pour in the brandy. Grease an 8-inch tin well, pour in the mixture and bake in a moderate oven for 40–50 minutes. Dust with icing sugar.

Kastana krokettes

Fried chestnut balls

4–6 Servings

2 lb. chestnuts
6 oz. sugar
½ pint milk
2 egg yolks
2 oz. chopped glacé
  cherries
2 oz. finely chopped
  candied peel

small piece cinnamon
2 oz. fine dried
  breadcrumbs
deep fat for frying
icing sugar
ground cinnamon

Cut a gash in the shell of the chestnuts and boil for 20 minutes. Remove the shells and brown skin and put the flesh in a pan with the milk, cinnamon and 3 tablespoons sugar. Boil gently until all the milk is absorbed. Discard the cinnamon and rub the chestnuts through a sieve. Mix in the rest of the sugar and the chopped peel and cherries, and working very lightly form into nut-sized balls. Dip in the beaten egg yolks and cover thickly in crumbs. Fry in plenty of smoking hot fat until golden brown. Drain on paper and sprinkle with icing sugar and cinnamon. (This quantity makes 25 balls.)

Halvas pascalinos

Halva Easter cake

6 oz. butter	*Syrup:*
6 oz. castor sugar	8 oz. sugar
4 eggs	$\frac{1}{4}$ pint water
juice and rind 1 orange	small stick cinnamon
10 oz. semolina	3 tablespoons orange
2 teaspoons baking	juice
powder	1 tablespoon lemon
4 oz. ground almonds	juice

Cream the butter and sugar until very light and fluffy.
Beat in the eggs one by one and stir in the juice and
grated rind of the orange. Add the semolina, baking
powder and ground almonds and mix until well blended.
Pour into a well greased cake tin and bake in a moderate
oven for 40 minutes, or until the top is golden. While
the cake is baking put the sugar, water, cinnamon and
orange and lemon juices to boil. Simmer until the syrup
thickens slightly. Remove the cake from the oven and
pour the hot syrup over it. Leave it to get cold and serve.
This is a very light and moist cake, but it does not
keep well.

Revani

Semolina cake

8 oz. butter	*Syrup:*
4 oz. sugar	1 lb. sugar
5 eggs	1 pint water
4 oz. flour	strip lemon peel
3 teaspoons baking	1 tablespoon brandy
powder	or Cointreau
8 oz. semolina	whipped cream
1 teaspoon grated	(optional)
lemon rind	

Beat the butter and sugar together until creamy. Whip the eggs and gradually add to the creamed mixture. Sift the flour, baking powder and semolina and add to the other ingredients with the grated lemon rind. Grease a baking tray well and spread the mixture to a depth of 2 inches. Bake in a moderate oven for 45 minutes, until firm and golden on top. Boil the sugar, water and lemon peel for 10 minutes, add the brandy or Cointreau and pour over the hot cake. When cold, cut into squares or diamonds and serve with whipped cream.

Yaourtopita

Yoghurt cake **(1)**

8 oz. flour	*Syrup:*
1 teaspoon bicarbonate of soda	12 oz. sugar
	$\frac{1}{4}$ pint white wine
pinch salt	2 tablespoons brandy
2 eggs, separated	1 small stick cinnamon
4 oz. castor sugar	
8 oz. yoghurt	

Sift the flour, bicarbonate of soda and salt into a mixing bowl. Beat the egg yolks with the sugar until thick and creamy and add to the flour. Stir until well blended and mix in the yoghurt and finally fold in the stiffly beaten egg whites. Turn the mixture into a well buttered cake tin and bake in a moderate oven for 35–40 minutes. While the cake is baking put the syrup ingredients in a small saucepan and boil for about 5 minutes. Pour the boiling syrup over the cake, as soon as you remove it from the oven. Serve when cold.

This cake makes a pleasant dessert, too, when topped with whipped cream and toasted sliced almonds.

Pita Yaourtiou

Yoghurt cake (2)

8 oz. butter
8 oz. castor sugar
1 carton yoghurt
5 eggs
1 lb. flour

pinch salt
2 teaspoons bicarbonate
  of soda
grated lemon rind
icing sugar

Soften the butter, add the sugar and cream until light and fluffy. Add the yoghurt, and when well blended add the eggs one by one, beating thoroughly after each addition. Sift the flour with the salt and bicarbonate of soda and fold into the creamed mixture. Stir in the grated lemon rind.

Bake in a moderate oven for about 1 hour. Dust with icing sugar.

Vasilopita

New Year's cake

2 tablespoons brewer's
  yeast
$\frac{1}{3}$ pint lukewarm milk
2$\frac{1}{2}$ lb. plain flour
1 teaspoon salt
8 oz. melted butter
8 eggs
10 oz. castor sugar

1 tablespoon grated
  orange rind
1 tablespoon grated
  lemon rind
1 egg yolk
4 tablespoons sesame
  seeds
3 oz. blanched almonds

Crumble the yeast into a basin, add the lukewarm milk and stir until dissolved. Add about 4 oz. of the flour and mix to a soft batter. Cover the basin with a thick cloth and leave in a warm place to 'sponge'. Sift the rest of the flour and salt into a large mixing bowl, make a well in the middle and add the melted (but not hot) butter, the eggs, sugar, orange and lemon rind and the risen yeast batter. Mix thoroughly to a soft sticky dough and then beat hard for a few minutes, until the mixture leaves the sides of the bowl clean. Cover with a sheet of grease-proof paper and a thick cloth and leave in a warm place to rise again to double its bulk. Turn the dough on to a well floured board and knead thoroughly. Cut off a small piece and put the rest into a buttered baking tin large enough to allow for further rising. The pita at this stage should be about 2 inches thick. Using your hands, roll the cut-off piece into a long rope. Divide this into four and shape into numerals to 'write' the number of the New Year on top of the cake. Cover as before and set mixture to rise until almost double its bulk. Beat the egg yolk with $\frac{1}{2}$ tablespoon water and brush the top of the cake, and using the back of a fork make patterns to decorate the edge, or snip with scissors. Sprinkle with the coarsely chopped almonds and the sesame seeds and bake in a moderately hot oven for about 1 hour. Before baking the Greeks push a gold or silver coin into the cake.

On New Year's day the Greeks celebrate also St. Basil's day, after whom this cake is named. It is St. Basil who brings the presents to the Greek children and not Santa Claus, as in other countries. As the clock strikes midnight on New Year's eve the head of the household cuts this traditional cake and the first slice is put aside for St. Basil. Then slices are cut for the members of the family present and absent alike and the search begins for the buried gold or silver coin. The finder will be assured of good luck throughout the coming year, and should the coin be in St. Basil's slice then the whole family will be blessed with good luck. St. Basil's portion and those of the absent relatives are usually given to the poor.

Tsourekia Pascalina

Easter buns

1 tablespoon aniseed	½ teaspoon salt
little water	3–4 eggs
1½ tablespoons yeast	6 oz. melted butter
¼ pint warm milk	8 oz. castor sugar
1½ lb. flour	1 egg yolk
½ tablespoon grated orange rind	3 oz. blanched almonds

Simmer the aniseed in a little water for 5 minutes. Strain and put aside 4 tablespoons of the liquid. Put the yeast in a small basin and mash it with a little of the lukewarm milk. Add 3 oz. of the flour and mix to a batter. Cover with a cloth and set in a warm place to prove. When the batter bubbles and is spongy the yeast mixture is ready. In the meantime sift the rest of the flour in a large mixing bowl, adding the salt and orange rind. Make a well in the middle and add the eggs, melted butter, sugar, yeast and the aniseed water. Mix until all the ingredients are well blended and work to a soft smooth dough. Cover the bowl with a sheet of greaseproof paper and a thick cloth and leave in a warm place until the dough has risen to double its bulk. Turn the dough on to a well floured board, knead lightly and break off even-sized pieces which you roll into long 'sausages'. Plait three of the 'sausages' to form the tsoureki, tucking the ends neatly under to prevent them from coming apart during baking. Arrange on a greased baking tray and set aside in a warm place to rise for the third time. Beat the egg yolk with a little water and glaze the buns. Sprinkle with the coarsely chopped almonds and bake in a moderately hot oven for 30 minutes. (This quantity makes 2–3 large buns.)

This is the traditional Easter bun. Sometimes, particularly among families with young children a scarlet egg is inserted in the middle of the bun before putting it in the oven. The eggs are first hard-boiled in water tinted with cochineal or other vegetable dye.

When the family go to the midnight service to celebrate the Resurrection the children always carry a scarlet egg in their pockets. When the priest pronounces the miracle of the resurrection with a jubilant '*Hristos Anesti*' (Christ is risen) and this is taken up by the congregation with an equally jubilant '*Alithos Anesti*' (Truly He is risen) the children break their eggs, smashing them against each other's. Round the breakfast table the members of the family will break more scarlet eggs and repeat the 'Christ is risen' to each other and wish everyone '*Kalo Pascha*' (Happy Easter). The royal family usually visits the barracks near Athens to crack Easter eggs with officers and men, to the accompaniment of more '*Hristos Anesti*'.

The origin of this custom is lost in legend but it is supposed to symbolize the smashing of the tomb and release of our Lord. It is known, of course, that the early Christians believed the egg to be full of blessings and by smashing it one frees these blessings. The dyeing of eggs dates back to well before the Christian era. Anyway, whatever the explanation is, Easter without scarlet eggs is unthinkable to a self-respecting Greek.

Karydata

Coffee walnuts

4 oz. ground walnuts	2–3 drops vanilla essence
8 oz. icing sugar	1 teaspoon rose-water
3–4 tablespoons very strong coffee	1 tablespoon granulated sugar

Mix the walnuts and icing sugar and gradually add the coffee and vanilla essence to form a solid mixture. Moisten your hands with the rose-water and form little balls, the size of a walnut. Roll in the granulated sugar and leave aside for a few hours to harden before putting away in an airtight tin. These karydata will keep for 2–3 weeks.

Myzithropita

Cheese cake

8 oz. cottage cheese
12 oz. sifted flour
4–6 oz. castor sugar
pinch salt
½ teaspoon bicarbonate
of soda
2 teaspoons baking
powder

3 oz. butter
2–3 oz. currants
2–3 oz. mixed candied
peel
2 eggs
2 tablespoons milk
icing sugar

Press the cottage cheese through a sieve. Put the flour, sugar, salt, bicarbonate of soda and baking powder in a mixing bowl and add the softened butter and cottage cheese. Rub well with your finger tips and add the currants and candied peel. Beat the eggs with the milk and stir into the mixture. When all the ingredients are well blended pat the mixture into a round roughly 10 inches across, fold this in two to make a turnover and place on a lightly greased baking tin. Bake in a moderate oven for about 1 hour. Sprinkle with icing sugar.

Koulourakia

Small sweet cakes

12 oz. sifted flour
6 oz. butter
4 oz. sugar
2 teaspoons grated
lemon rind

1 egg
1 teaspoon bicarbonate
of soda
2 tablespoons brandy
or sherry

Sieve the flour into a basin, rub in the butter and add the sugar, lemon rind and beaten egg. Dissolve the soda in the brandy or sherry and stir into the other ingredients. The dough should be firm but pliable. If too stiff add a few drops of water, if slack add a little more flour. Cut off pieces and roll with your hands into long rope-like strips about the thickness and size of your little finger. Take two strips and twist them round and round lengthwise, pressing the two ends well. Cut these into 4-inch lengths and place on a greased baking sheet not too close together. Bake for 12–15 minutes in a hot oven.

Koulourakia me soussami

Small cakes with sesame seeds

6–8 oz. butter
6–8 oz. sugar
2 eggs
1½ lb. flour

1 teaspoon baking powder
pinch salt
2 tablespoons sesame
seeds

Soften the butter, add the sugar and beat until very light and fluffy. Add the 2 yolks and 1 egg white and beat for 5 minutes. Sieve the flour with the baking powder and salt and add to the creamed mixture. Work the mixture with your hand to make a firm, but not stiff, dough. Cut off pieces and roll these into sausages ¼–½ inch thick. Shape these into bracelet-sized rings. Place on a greased baking sheet, brush with lightly beaten egg white and sprinkle liberally with the sesame seeds. Bake in a fairly hot oven for 15–20 minutes or until the seeds are golden brown.

Pita nistisimi

Lenten cake

8 oz. sifted flour
4 oz. castor sugar
pinch salt
3 teaspoons baking
  powder

8 tablespoons orange
  juice
4 oz. ground walnuts
grated rind 1 orange
$\frac{1}{2}$ teaspoon olive oil

Put the flour, sugar, salt and baking powder in a basin and mix well. Make a well in the middle and gradually add the orange juice, stirring all the while. When the mixture is smooth stir in the ground walnuts and the orange rind. Grease a shallow, oblong tin with the oil and pour in the batter. Bake in a moderate oven for 50 minutes. This cake should be a day old before slicing.

Kourabiedes

Greek shortbread **(1)**

8 oz. unsalted butter
2 oz. castor sugar
1 lb. flour
1 teaspoon bicarbonate
  of soda

cloves
orange flower water
icing sugar

Beat the butter for 10 minutes, preferably with your hand, until very light and creamy. Add the sugar and continue to beat until there is no trace of sugar. Sift the flour with the bicarbonate of soda and gradually mix into the butter. Knead well with your fingers. The dough should be soft and pliable and should leave the basin clean. Form into biscuit shapes or into very small 'sausages' and twist the two ends to form the letter S. Insert a clove in each of the kourabiedes, arrange in rows on a floured baking tray, not too close together, and cook in a moderate oven for 20 minutes. They should be cooked through, but not coloured. While still hot sprinkle with orange-flower water and roll in icing sugar to cover them thickly. These cakes will keep for a few weeks in an airtight container.

Kourabiedes

Greek shortbread (2)

8 oz. unsalted butter
2 oz. castor sugar
1 tablespoon ouzo
  or brandy
1 egg yolk

12–16 oz. flour
½ teaspoon baking
  powder
orange-flower water
8 oz. icing sugar

Cream the butter, add the sugar and beat for at least 15 minutes. The texture of the kourabiedes depends largely on this preliminary beating. Mix in the ouzo or brandy and egg yolk and gradually work in enough sifted flour and baking powder to make a firm but smooth and pliable dough, which should leave the sides of the bowl clean. Cut off small pieces and shape into ovals, rounds or crescent shapes. Bake in a moderate oven for 20 minutes, by which time they should be cooked through, but not coloured. Remove from the oven and while still hot sprinkle with orange-flower water and cover thickly with sifted icing sugar. Cool and keep in airtight tins. (This quantity makes 20–25 pieces of shortbread.)

Koulourakia portokaliou

Little orange cakes

1¼ lb. flour
4 oz. melted butter
  or margarine
1½ teaspoons bicarbonate
  of ammonia
2 tablespoons
  lukewarm water

4 oz. sugar
4 tablespoons honey
¼ pint orange juice
1 tablespoon grated
  orange rind

Sieve the flour into a mixing bowl. Make a well in the middle and pour in the hot butter or margarine. Rub with your fingers until well blended. Dissolve the ammonia in the lukewarm water and add to the flour, also the sugar, honey, orange juice and orange rind. Mix well and knead to make a soft dough. Form into small fancy shapes or use a biscuit cutter. Arrange well apart on a greased baking tin, and bake in a hot oven for 10–15 minutes, according to size.

Koulourakia kanellas

Little cinnamon cakes

1¼ lb. flour
1 tablespoon ground
  cinnamon
1 teaspoon ground cloves
4 oz. butter or margarine

1 teaspoon bicarbonate
  of ammonia
3 oz. milk
2 eggs, separated
4 oz. sugar

Sieve the flour into a mixing bowl and add the spices. Melt the butter and when hot pour into the flour. Mix well with your fingertips. Dissolve the ammonia in the lukewarm milk and stir it into the flour. Beat the egg yolks with the sugar and add to the other ingredients, and finally fold in the stiffly beaten egg whites. Mix thoroughly to a soft but not sticky dough. Form into fancy shapes or rings and bake in a moderate oven for about 20 minutes.

Kourabiedes me amygdalo

Shortbread with almonds

10 oz. butter
4 oz. castor sugar
1 egg yolk
4 oz. ground almonds
4 oz. roasted chopped
  almonds

1 teaspoon baking
  powder
1 tablespoon brandy
vanilla
1¼ lb. flour (approx.)
icing sugar

Beat the butter and sugar for at least 15 minutes. Add the egg yolk, ground almonds, finely chopped roasted almonds, and when these are well blended dilute the baking powder in the brandy, add a little vanilla essence to taste and stir into the creamed mixture. Sift the flour and add to the other ingredients. Knead well. The dough should be firm but pliable. Shape in ovals, rounds or fingers. Place on a floured baking sheet, not too close together, and cook in a moderate oven for 20–25 minutes. While still hot cover thickly in icing sugar.

Glykisma psighiou

Refrigerator cake

8 oz. margarine
8 oz. castor sugar
3 level tablespoons
  cocoa
2 fresh eggs

12 oz. *petit-beurre*
  biscuits
1 tablespoon brandy
2–3 oz. toasted
  almonds

Melt the margarine over boiling water, but do not allow it to become hot. Stir in the sugar, cocoa and beaten eggs, and mix to a smooth cream. Break the biscuits into tiny pieces and chop the almonds coarsely. Add to the cocoa cream with the brandy and mix until all the ingredients are well blended. Empty the mixture on to a sheet of thick greaseproof paper and roll up like a Swiss roll. Twist the ends tightly and place in a refrigerator for 4–5 hours, or in a cold place overnight, to set.

Halvas me alevri

Halva with nuts and sultanas

12 oz. sugar	2 tablespoons coarsely
1 pint water	chopped walnuts
4 oz. honey	2 tablespoons pine
1 stick cinnamon	kernels
3 cloves	2 tablespoons sultanas
$\frac{1}{4}$ pint olive oil	1 teaspoon ground
(or butter)	cinnamon
8 oz. flour	2 teaspoons sugar

Boil the sugar, water, honey, stick of cinnamon and cloves to a thin syrup. Heat the oil or butter and when bubbling gradually stir in the flour. Keep stirring with a wooden spoon until the flour starts to colour and add the nuts, pine kernels and sultanas. Continue to cook over a very gentle heat until the flour turns light brown. Remove from the heat and pour in the hot, strained syrup. Cover the saucepan with a napkin and a lid and place in a very low oven, or at the back of the stove until all the syrup has been absorbed. Stir well and pack into a mould. Turn on to a glass dish and sprinkle with cinnamon and sugar. This may be eaten hot or cold.

Amygdaloto

Almond cake

4 eggs	dried breadcrumbs
1 lb. castor sugar	orange-flower water
1 lb. ground almonds	icing sugar
grated orange or lemon rind	

Separate the eggs and beat the yolks with the sugar until very light and creamy. Gradually add the almonds, beating all the while, and mix in the flavouring. When these ingredients are thoroughly blended fold in the stiffly beaten egg whites. Butter a sandwich tin and sprinkle with dried breadcrumbs. Pour in the mixture, which should not be more than ⅔ full, cover the top of the tin with a sheet of paper and bake in a moderate oven for 35–40 minutes. Cool, turn on to a dish and sprinkle with orange-flower water and icing sugar.

Roulo me chantilly

Roll with whipped cream

5 eggs, separated	1 teaspoon baking powder
6 oz. castor sugar	2 tablespoons brandy
3 heaped tablespoons cocoa	whipped cream
	icing sugar

Beat the egg yolks with the sugar until light and fluffy. Add the cocoa, previously sifted with the baking powder, and stir in the brandy. Mix thoroughly and add the stiffly beaten egg whites. Line a Swiss roll tin with oiled greaseproof paper and pour in the mixture. Bake in a very moderate oven for 10 minutes. Remove the paper, cool slightly and spread with the cream. Roll up lightly and place in refrigerator. Before serving sprinkle with icing sugar.

Pita portokaliou

Orange cake

6 oz. butter	2 oz. dates
6 oz. sugar	2 oz. walnuts
3 eggs	12 oz. self-raising flour
1 teaspoon bicarbonate	vanilla essence
of soda	2 large juicy oranges
½ bottle yoghurt	8 oz. sugar

Beat the butter and the 6 oz. of sugar until light and fluffy. Beat in the eggs one at a time. Mix the baking soda with the yoghurt and add to the creamed mixture. Chop the dates and walnuts coarsely and add to the flour with vanilla essence to taste and the grated rind of the oranges. Pour the mixture in a well greased tin and bake in a moderate oven for about 1 hour. In the meantime, melt the 8 oz. sugar in the orange juice over gentle heat. Boil steadily for 5 minutes. Remove the cake from the oven and pour the hot syrup over it. Leave to get cold. For a more luscious cake cover the top with whipped cream.

Kopenhayi

Kopenhagen

5 oz. almonds	*Syrup:*
5 oz. toasted	1 lb. sugar
breadcrumbs	1 pint water
grated rind ½ lemon	1 teaspoon lemon
1 teaspoon cinnamon	juice
3–4 tablespoons brandy	lemon peel
5 eggs	2–3 cloves
4 oz. sugar	
4 oz. butter	
8 oz. phyllo pastry	

Grind the almonds without first blanching them and put in a basin with the toasted breadcrumbs, grated rind of ½ lemon and the cinnamon. Pour over the brandy and stir until thoroughly blended. Separate the eggs and put the yolks in a bowl with 4 oz. sugar. Beat until thick and creamy. Whip the egg whites until stiff and mix with the yolks. Add to the almond mixture and stir well. Grease a baking tin with melted butter and line with one sheet of pastry. Brush this with melted butter and continue in this way until you have used 4 oz. of pastry, i.e. roughly 6 sheets. Spread the almond mixture evenly and cover with the rest of the pastry, spreading each sheet separately with melted butter. With a really sharp knife score the surface to make strips 1½ × 4 inches long. Bake in a moderate oven for 45 minutes. In the meantime, melt the sugar with the 1 pint water and 1 teaspoon lemon juice. Add the cloves and lemon juice to taste, and boil steadily until it forms a fairly thick syrup. Remove the kopenhayi from the oven and spoon the syrup all over it. Cover with a napkin and cool before serving.

Note:

This cake was created in honour of King George I of the Hellenes, who was a Danish prince before his ascension to the Greek throne.

Melopita sifnaiki

Sifnos honeycake

6 SERVINGS

pinch salt
6 oz. sifted flour
2 oz. butter
1 egg yolk
8–10 oz. curd cheese

2 tablespoons honey
2 eggs
2 teaspoons cinnamon
1 tablespoon castor
   sugar

Add the pinch of salt to the sifted flour and rub in the butter. Bind with the egg yolk and roll out thinly. Line a greased sandwich tin with the pastry, leave in a cool place and prepare the filling. Sieve the curd cheese and mix in the honey, the 2 well-beaten eggs, one teaspoon cinnamon and the sugar. Spread the mixture in the pastry case and bake in a moderate oven for 40–45 minutes, or until golden brown on top. Sprinkle with the rest of the cinnamon and serve cold.

This is the traditional cake eaten at Easter on the Island of Sifnos.

Karydopita

Walnut cake

12 oz. shelled walnuts
12 oz. sugar
6 tablespoons flour
2 oz. grated chocolate

6 eggs, separated
2 teaspoons cinnamon
pinch salt

Chop or grind the walnuts coarsely and mix with half the quantity of sugar. Add the sifted flour and grated chocolate. Separate the eggs and beat the yolks with the rest of the sugar until light and creamy. Add the cinnamon and pour into the walnut mixture. Whip the egg whites with a pinch of salt until they form peaks and fold carefully into the other ingredients. Grease and flour a cake tin, turn in the mixture and bake in a moderate oven for 35–40 minutes.

Kastanato

Chestnut gâteau

12 SERVINGS

2 lb. chestnuts	4 oz. butter
1 lb. sugar	6 oz. plain chocolate
¼ pint water	whipped cream
1 teaspoon vanilla essence	

Peel the chestnuts and put them in water to boil until tender. Remove the skin and put through a 'mouli' sieve or a potato masher. Melt the sugar in about ¼ pint water and boil until it forms a fairly thick syrup. Add the chestnut purée and the vanilla and stir well. In the meantime melt the butter and chocolate over gentle heat and when ready pour into the chestnut mixture. Cook slowly for 30 minutes, stirring continuously. Grease a fancy mould or any other dish and pour in the mixture. Press well and leave it to set for 12 hours in a cold place, or less in a refrigerator. Decorate with whipped cream.

Pasteli

Honey and sesame seed wafers

1 lb. honey	1 lb. sesame seeds

Put the honey in a heavy saucepan and bring to the boil. Add the sesame seeds and cook gently until large bubbles appear on the surface. Test for a set. If a drop in a tumbler of cold water retains its shape the pasteli is ready. If at all in doubt, it is better to over-cook. Pour on to a well oiled tray or marble slab and spread with a spatula to ¼ inch thickness. When cold cut into wafers and store in an airtight container.

These wafers are delicious for those with a really sweet tooth. The sesame seeds can be bought in health stores and when cooked they taste like roasted almonds.

Paximadakia

Rusks

1½ lb. flour	2 eggs
2 teaspoons baking powder	4 oz. castor sugar
1 tablespoon caraway seeds	¼ pint lukewarm milk (scant)
4 oz. margarine or butter	little egg yolk

Sift the flour with the baking powder and add the caraway seeds. Heat the butter and pour into the flour; knead with your fingertips until well blended. Lightly beat the eggs with the sugar, gradually add the tepid milk and stir into the flour. Knead well to a firm dough and roll with your hands to form 2 thick 'sausages', about 2–2½ inches across. Place on a greased baking tray, brush well with the egg yolk, previously beaten with a few drops of water, and bake in a moderate oven for 20 minutes. When the rolls are quite cold, slice with a very sharp knife and put in the oven to brown on both sides.

Instead of caraway seeds, you can use grated lemon or orange rind and a few currants. These paximadakia keep very well in an airtight tin.

Bougatsa

Heavenly slices

1½ pints milk	12 oz. phyllo pastry
4 oz. semolina	4 oz. melted butter
4 eggs	6 oz. icing sugar
8 oz. sugar	1 tablespoon cinnamon
vanilla essence	

Heat the milk and sprinkle in the semolina. Cook over a low heat until the mixture thickens, stirring continuously. Lightly beat the eggs with the sugar and vanilla essence and carefully stir into the semolina. Cook for a further 5 minutes and remove from the heat. Cool the mixture, stirring occasionally to prevent skin forming on top. In the meantime butter an oblong tin slightly smaller than your pastry sheets, and line it with 8–9 sheets, each one brushed separately with melted butter. Pour in the semolina custard and spread evenly. Turn the edges of the pastry over to enclose the custard and brush the edges with a little melted butter. Cover with the rest of the pastry, again brushing each sheet separately with butter. With kitchen scissors or a very sharp knife cut off the surplus pastry. Brush the top layer with the rest of the butter and score into squares or diamonds. Bake in a moderate oven for 35–40 minutes and cover thickly with icing sugar and cinnamon while still hot. Cut the squares right through and serve hot.

Diples
Fried pastry knots

10–12 oz. flour	4 tablespoons Cointreau
1 teaspoon baking powder	deep oil for frying
	honey
3 eggs	ground walnuts
2 tablespoons castor sugar	

Sift the flour and baking powder into a basin and make a well in the middle. Beat the eggs with the sugar and gradually add the liqueur. Stir the mixture into the flour and work to a stiff dough — if too stiff add a little orange juice or water. Leave for 30 minutes. Turn the dough on to a floured pastry board and roll to $\frac{1}{8}$ inch thick. Cut strips about 1 inch wide and tie into a knot. Fry in plenty of smoking hot oil until golden brown. Dilute some honey in warm water, mix in the walnuts and pour over the diples which you have previously drained on absorbent paper. Alternatively, sprinkle the pastries with cinnamon and icing sugar.

Skaltsounakia

Nut and honey turnovers

8 oz. shelled walnuts
6 oz. shelled almonds
2 tablespoons castor
sugar
1 tablespoon cinnamon
and cloves, mixed
honey

Pastry:

1 lb. flour
pinch salt
1 teaspoon baking
powder
6 oz. butter
¼ pint water (scant)

orange-flower water
icing sugar

Put the nuts through the mincer and add the sugar, spices and enough honey to bind all the ingredients together. Add the salt and baking powder to the flour, mix in the butter and bind with the water to make a stiff dough. Roll out ¼ inch thick and cut out with a scone cutter. Put one spoonful of the mixture on half the round, dampen the edge and fold over, pressing well. Place on a greased baking sheet and bake in a moderate oven for 20–25 minutes, until a very pale biscuit colour. Cool slightly, sprinkle with the orange-flower water and cover thickly with icing sugar.

Svingoi

Sweet puffs

½ pint water
½ teaspoon salt
4 oz. butter
strip of lemon peel
6 oz. flour
4 eggs
deep fat for frying

Syrup:

8 oz. sugar
2–3 tablespoons honey
8 tablespoons water
small piece cinnamon
2 cloves
2 tablespoons brandy
or liqueur
little icing sugar

Put the water, salt, butter and lemon peel in a small pan and boil for 1–2 minutes. Remove the pan from the heat and throw in the flour, mixing quickly with a wooden spoon. Return the pan to the heat and cook gently until the mixture is smooth and elastic and leaves the sides of the pan clean. Cool slightly and add the eggs one at a time, beating continuously and hard for a few minutes. Have ready a pan of hot fat and drop teaspoonfuls of the mixture. Cook slowly at first and when well puffed increase the heat until crisp and golden brown. Remove with a perforated spoon on to kitchen paper to drain. In the meantime boil the sugar, honey, water and spices for 8–10 minutes to a moderately thick syrup. Discard the spices and stir in the brandy. Sprinkle the puffs with icing sugar and serve the syrup separately. (This quantity makes 25–30 puffs.)

Pita me verikoka

Apricot tart

Pastry:

8 oz. flour
½ teaspoon baking powder
2 teaspoons sugar
5 oz. butter
1 egg yolk
1 tablespoon brandy

Filling:

3 tablespoons apricot jam
1 lb. apricots
3 tablespoons sugar
1 tablespoon melted butter
1 egg white

Sieve the flour with the baking powder and add the sugar. Rub in the butter and bind with the egg yolk and brandy to a soft dough. Roll out ¼ inch thick and cut into 2 rounds. Place one round in a greased baking tin, prick well with a fork and bake in a hot oven for about 10 minutes. Remove from the oven and spread with the apricot jam. Stone and halve the apricots and arrange neatly on the jam. Sprinkle with sugar and the melted butter. Cover with the round of pastry, brush with egg white and press to seal the edges. Return to a moderate oven for a further 25–30 minutes.

Mylopita

Apple tart

8 oz. flour
1 teaspoon baking powder
2 teaspoons castor sugar
4 oz. butter or margarine
1 egg yolk
1 tablespoon brandy
1½ lb. cooking apples

2 tablespoons sugar
1 tablespoon cinnamon
(or to taste)
1 egg white
1 tablespoon melted
butter

Sieve the flour with the baking powder and mix in the 2 teaspoons sugar. Rub in the butter and mix to a soft dough with the lightly beaten egg yolk and brandy. Roll out ¼ inch thick and line a large greased pie plate. Prick the bottom with a fork and put in a hot oven for 10 minutes. In the meantime, peel and cut the apples into small pieces. Mix with 2 tablespoons sugar, cinnamon and stiffly beaten egg white and spread on the partly cooked pastry shell. Pour the melted butter on top and return to a moderate oven for a further 20–25 minutes to finish cooking.

Mizithropita me meli

Cottage cheese and honey pie

4–6 SERVINGS

Pastry:
6 oz. flour
pinch salt
3 oz. butter
or margarine
water to mix

Filling:
1 lb. cottage cheese
6 oz. honey
4 oz. sugar
4–5 eggs
1½ tablespoons cinnamon
(or to taste)

Sieve flour with salt, rub in the butter until it looks like fine breadcrumbs and mix with water to a pliable paste. Roll out to a thickness of less than ¼ inch and line a well greased sandwich tin. Mix the cottage cheese with honey and sugar, add the lightly beaten eggs and half the cinnamon. When the mixture is thoroughly blended rub through a fine sieve and spread into the sandwich tin. Bake in a moderate oven for 40–45 minutes. Dredge with icing sugar and the rest of the cinnamon. This pie can be eaten warm or cold.

Loukoumades

Honey puffs

10 oz. flour	*Syrup:*
½ teaspoon salt	4 oz. honey
½ tablespoon brewer's yeast	6 oz. sugar
	⅓ pint water
deep oil for frying	cinnamon
lukewarm water	

Sift the flour and salt in a mixing bowl. Make a well in the middle and add the yeast, previously dissolved in a little lukewarm water. Stir until the flour and yeast are well mixed and gradually add enough lukewarm water to make a medium thick batter. Beat well for a few minutes, cover the bowl with a thick cloth and leave in a warm place until the dough doubles its bulk. Have ready a pan of smoking hot oil, dip your hands in cold water, take some of the dough and squeeze between thumb and first finger to form a bubble. Drop this in the fat and fry until well puffed and golden brown. In the meantime, boil the honey, sugar and water to a fairly thick syrup and pour over the hot honey puffs. Sprinkle with cinnamon and serve.

Bourekakia me karydi

Rolls stuffed with walnuts

8 SERVINGS

8 oz. ground walnuts
4 oz. toasted
  breadcrumbs
4 oz. sugar
1 teaspoon cinnamon
pinch nutmeg
pinch grated lemon rind
1 lb. phyllo pastry
6 oz. melted butter

Syrup:
1 lb. sugar
½ pint water
1 lemon

Mix together the walnuts, breadcrumbs, sugar, spices and lemon rind. Cut the pastry into strips 4 × 12 inches. Brush each strip with melted butter and fold in two lengthwise. Put a spoonful of the mixture on one end and roll up like a Swiss roll. Arrange the rolls on a greased baking tin and bake in a moderate oven for 25–30 minutes. Remove from the oven and let them cool, while you prepare the syrup. Put the sugar, water and lemon juice to boil. Simmer for 10 minutes, or until it forms a moderately thick syrup. Pour the syrup over the rolls, cover with a napkin and leave for a few hours before serving.

Kataifi me krema

Kataifi pastry with custard filling

1½ pints milk
4 oz. sugar
6 oz. fine semolina
2 oz. butter
vanilla to taste
4 eggs
1 lb. kataifi pastry*

6 oz. melted butter
1 lb. sugar
1¼ pints water
lemon juice
lemon peel
cinnamon powder

* Kataifi pastry cannot be made at home. It is made by professional pastrycooks and can be bought in Greek and Cypriot shops in most of the larger towns. It is sold in 1-lb. packets.

First prepare the filling. Bring the milk to boiling point, add the sugar and sprinkle in the semolina. Cook slowly until the mixture thickens, stirring all the time to prevent it from catching to the bottom of the pan. Remove from the heat and stir in the 2 oz. butter and the vanilla flavouring and allow to cool slightly before adding the well beaten eggs. Spread half the pastry in a buttered shallow baking tin, spoon over it half the melted butter and pour in the filling. Cover with the remaining pastry and pour over the rest of the melted butter, spreading it evenly. Bake in a moderate oven for 40–45 minutes. In the meantime, boil the sugar, water, lemon juice and peel for about 10 minutes, or until the syrup thickens slightly, and pour this over the pastry as soon as you remove it from the oven. Cover the tin with a napkin and allow it to cool before cutting into 12–14 serving portions. Sprinkle with cinnamon to taste.

Koulourakia me tyri

Rich cheese biscuits

1 lb. flour	8 oz. butter
1 teaspoon salt	2 eggs
1 teaspoon baking powder	1 tablespoon milk
6 oz. grated Parmesan cheese	

Sift the flour with the salt and baking powder and add the grated cheese. Melt the butter, allow to cool and mix into the flour, using the tips of your fingers. Add the lightly beaten eggs and work to a smooth, firm dough. Cut off small pieces and shape. Brush with milk and bake in a moderate oven for 15–20 minutes.

Kataifi me karydi

Kataifi pastry stuffed with walnuts

1 lb. kataifi pastry*	*Syrup:*
8 oz. melted butter	1 lb. sugar
12 oz. ground walnuts	1¼ pints water
4 oz. sugar	1 teaspoon lemon juice
3 teaspoons cinnamon	strip lemon peel
1–2 eggs	
* See page 235	

Butter a large shallow baking dish and spread half the kataifi pastry evenly. Pour over this half the melted butter. Mix in a bowl the walnuts, 4 oz. sugar and cinnamon and bind with the lightly beaten egg. Spread this carefully on top of the pastry and cover with the remaining kataifi. Pour over the rest of the melted butter and bake in a moderate oven for 40–45 minutes. In the meantime, boil the sugar with the water, lemon juice and lemon peel until you have a moderately thick syrup. Cool the kataifi and pour the boiling syrup over it. Cover immediately with a napkin and leave until all the syrup has been absorbed. Cut into squares or oblongs to serve. It keeps for a week or more. (This quantity makes 20–24 pieces.)

Galaktoboureko

Cream slices

1½ pints milk	1 lb phyllo pastry
6 oz. semolina	6–8 oz. melted butter
5 eggs	1½ lb. sugar
6 oz. sugar	1 pint water
vanilla to taste	lemon peel
1½ oz. butter	1 teaspoon lemon juice

Bring the milk to boiling point, add the semolina, stirring continuously with a wooden spoon until the mixture thickens. Beat the eggs with the sugar and vanilla until thick and creamy. Remove the pan from the heat and stir in the egg mixture. Add the 1½ oz. butter and mix thoroughly. Allow the mixture to cool, stirring occasionally to prevent a skin forming. Butter a rectangular baking tin slightly smaller than your phyllo pastry and line with half the pastry, brushing each sheet separately with melted butter. Spread the semolina cream evenly and turn the edges of the pastry over to enclose the filling. Cover with the remaining pastry each sheet treated as before. With a sharp knife cut off the surplus pastry and score through the top layers into serving slices. Brush with the rest of the butter, sprinkle with a little water and bake in a moderate oven for 35–40 minutes. In the meantime, boil the sugar with the water, lemon peel and lemon juice for 8–10 minutes and pour this syrup over the galaktoboureko as soon as you remove it from the oven. Cool and serve.

Note:

Some cooks add 1 tablespoon brandy to the syrup instead of the lemon peel. (This quantity makes 24 slices.)

Jams and Preserves

One of the specialities of Greek cooking is the lovely and rather unusual jams and preserves, which every housewife takes pride in making. When you visit a Greek household you will be offered a tray on which is placed a bowl of jam, a glass of water and a small glass of cognac or liqueur, followed by a cup of Turkish coffee. This is Greek hospitality and foreigners find the custom rather pleasant and quaint, but it can be embarrassing, too, when faced with it for the first time. The story goes that an English visitor after eating the best part of the contents of the bowl, turned apologetically to his hostess and declared that he could not possibly eat the lot! The custom is to take one spoonful of jam only and then drink the water.

Some of the preserves can be made quite easily in England and I have selected recipes which I know would be suitable for the tea-table.

To test *if jam is set, drop a little in a glass of cold water. It should retain its shape.*

Glyko hourmades

Date jam

1 lb. dates	small piece cinnamon
2 oz. blanched almonds	2–3 cloves
12 oz. sugar	$\frac{1}{2}$ lemon
water	

Choose small, light-coloured dates: the boxed ones are quite suitable. Carefully remove the stone and insert a blanched almond in the cavity. Put the sugar in a pan and just enough water to dissolve it. Add the cinnamon and the cloves and bring to the boil. Boil fast for 5 minutes and add the dates. Lower the heat and continue cooking for 10–15 minutes. Remove the dates with a perforated spoon and strain the syrup. Return to the pan, add the lemon juice and boil fast until it sets (see above). Add the dates and remove from the heat. Cool and pour into sterilized jars. Cover in the usual way.

Kydoni peltes

Quince jelly

3 lb. quinces	1 teaspoon lemon
2 quarts water	juice
2 lb. preserving	vanilla pod
sugar	(optional)

Wash and peel the fruit. Cut into thick slices and remove the pips. Put the quinces in a large saucepan, cover with water and add the peel and pips tied in a muslin bag. Simmer for 1–1½ hours or until the fruit is very tender. Remove the pan from the heat, squeeze the muslin bag lightly and discard the contents. Turn the contents of the pan into a jelly bag and let it drip over a basin, without squeezing the bag which would make the jelly cloudy. Measure the liquid and return to the pan, but do not discard the pulp, which can be turned into a delicious sweetmeat. Bring the liquid to the boil, add the sugar and vanilla, and boil fast until the jelly sets when tested (see page 239). Just before setting point is reached add the lemon juice, skim well. Pour into sterilized jars and allow the jelly to get cold before sealing.

Note:

If you have no jelly bag, you can strain the fruit through several thicknesses of muslin, tied by the four corners to the legs of an upturned chair or stool.

Kydoni trifto

Quince preserve

2 lb. quinces	1 tablespoon lemon
2 lb. sugar	juice
½ pint water	2 tablespoons pine
(approximately)	kernels

Peel the quinces and grate coarsely. Put the sugar and water in a preserving pan and bring to the boil. Add the quinces and cook steadily until the mixture begins to thicken. Add the lemon juice and boil fast until it sets (see page 239). Just before setting point is reached stir in the pine kernels. Pour in sterilized warm dry jars and seal in the usual way.

Kydonopasto

Quince paste

4 lb. quinces	small piece cinnamon
water	bay leaves
1 lb. sugar	brandy (optional)
4 oz. honey	crystallized sugar
4 oz. finely chopped	(optional)
roasted almonds	

Peel and core the quinces. Cut into small pieces and barely cover with water. Simmer gently until very tender and rub through a sieve. Return to the pan with the sugar, honey, almonds and piece of cinnamon. Bring to the boil and cook steadily until the paste comes away from the sides of the pan, about 40–60 minutes. Grease lightly a shllaow tin with either almond or olive oil and pour the mixture in it. Spread with a spatula to a thickness of 1½–2 inches and leave it to cool. Cut into squares or small fancy shapes and leave in the sun for 1–2 days to harden, or in a very cool oven for a few hours. When completely dry, put in layers in an airtight tin with a bay leaf or two between each layer. To make them more attractive you can sprinkle them with a few drops of brandy or liqueur and roll them in crystallized sugar before packing in the tin.

Glyko triandaphyllo

Rose petal jam

1 lb. fresh roses	2 teaspoons lemon
2 lb. sugar	juice
½ pint water	

Choose red cabbage-type roses while the dew is still upon them and strip off the petals. Cut off the hard white base, sprinkle with 1 tablespoon sugar and mix well. Cover and leave overnight. Next day put the sugar with the water to boil. When all the sugar is dissolved skim well and boil fast until the syrup is beginning to thicken. Add the rose petals and bring to the boil again. Cook steadily until the jam thickens and the petals look transparent — about 30–40 minutes. Just before removing from the heat, add the lemon juice and stir. Pour into small sterilized jars and cover when cold.

Vyssino glyko

Black cherry jam

3 lb. sour black cherries	¼ pint water
4 lb. preserving sugar	1 tablespoon lemon juice

Wash the cherries. Remove stalks and stones with a needle or a sterilized hairpin, but be careful to keep the fruit whole. Put in a preserving pan with the sugar and water and heat slowly until the sugar is completely dissolved. Bring to the boil and boil fast for 40 minutes to 1 hour, or until the cherries are tender and the syrup thick like honey. Skim off the scum and pour in the lemon juice. Test to see if setting point is reached (see page 239). Pour in sterilized jars and seal in the usual way.

1 tablespoon of the syrup diluted with iced or mineral water makes a very refreshing drink.

Stafyli glyko

Grape jam

3 lb. seedless grapes
2 lb. preserving sugar
1 teaspoon lemon juice
$\frac{1}{3}$ pint water
vanilla

Choose firm sound grapes, strip and wash well. Put the sugar and water in a preserving pan and bring gradually to the boil. Boil steadily until the syrup thickens and drop in the grapes. Increase the heat and boil fast until the jam sets when tested (see page 239). Skim, add the lemon juice and bring to the boil once. Add the vanilla and allow the jam to get cool before pouring into small sterilized jars. Cover in the usual way.

Sykaki glyko

Green fig jam

$1\frac{1}{2}$ lb. tiny unripe green figs
blanched almonds
$1\frac{1}{2}$ lb. preserving sugar
9 tablespoons water
2 oz. glucose
vanilla pod or powder

Remove the stalk from the figs and wash well. Put in a large saucepan, cover with water and boil steadily until the fruit is tender. Drain thoroughly and when cool enough to handle insert one blanched almond in the hole made by the stalk and push down well. Bring the sugar with the 9 tablespoons water gradually to the boil and after 5 minutes add the figs. Boil fast for a further 5 minutes, remove the pan from the heat and leave overnight. Next day bring to the boil again, skim well and add the glucose and vanilla. Boil fast until the jam sets when tested (see page 239). Remove vanilla pod. Cool and seal in sterilized jars.

Nerandji glyko

Orange peel preserve

1½ lb. peel of bitter oranges	½ pint water
1¾ lb. preserving sugar	2 oz. glucose

Choose large thick-skinned fruit and grate lightly to remove the zest. Rinse and separate each orange into 8 sections. Remove the peel of each section neatly and roll up into a tight roll. Using a darning needle, thread 18–20 rolls together and tie securely. Put them in a large saucepan, cover with plenty of cold water and boil steadily until the peel is very tender. Drain, cover them with fresh water and leave them for 10 hours, changing the water at least twice. Remove into a collander to drain. In the meantime, put the sugar with ½ pint of water in a preserving pan and gradually bring to the boil. Boil for 5 minutes and throw in the orange rolls. Remove the pan from the heat after a further 5 minutes boiling and leave overnight. Next day bring the contents of the pan to the boil again, add the glucose and continue cooking until the jam sets when tested (see page 239). Cool, pour into sterilized jars and seal in the usual way.

Glyko fraoulas

Strawberry jam

2 lb. small strawberries	1 lemon
2 lb. sugar	2 tablespoons brandy

Remove stalks and hulls. Put the fruit and sugar into a basin, add the lemon juice and brandy and mix very lightly to avoid crushing the strawberries. Cover and leave overnight. Next day transfer to a preserving pan, bring quickly to boil and continue boiling steadily for about 20–30 minutes or until the jam sets when tested (see page 239). Skim well and pour into sterilized jars. Cover when completely cold.

Domates glyko

Tomato jam

1½ lb. tomatoes
water
1½ lb. preserving sugar
blanched almonds

1 teaspoon lemon juice
vanilla essence
6 tablespoons sugar

Pick very small, firm tomatoes and plunge in boiling water for one minute. Peel and spread out on to a large dish. Sprinkle with the 6 tablespoons sugar and leave for 24 hours. Put the liquid from the tomatoes into a pan, add a scant ⅛ pint water and the sugar and stir over gentle heat until the sugar is dissolved. Bring to the boil and boil fast for 15 minutes. Insert one blanched almond in each tomato and drop these in the boiling syrup. Boil for 2–3 minutes and remove the pan from the heat. Leave for 24 hours. Put the pan on the heat again, bring to the boil and add the lemon juice and vanilla. Boil steadily until the jam sets when tested (see page 239). Cool and pour in sterilized jars. Seal when cold in the usual way.

Glyko anthos lemonias

Lemon blossom preserve

1 lb. lemon blossom
3 lb. preserving sugar

1 pint water
1 tablespoon lemon juice

Mix the lemon blossom with two tablespoons sugar, cover and leave overnight. Next day put the rest of the sugar in the preserving pan, cover with the water and lemon juice and bring slowly to boil until all the sugar is dissolved. Boil steadily for 5 minutes and add the lemon blossom. Continue cooking until the jam thickens and the blossom becomes transparent. It should be the consistency of honey. Pour in sterilized warm dry jars and seal when completely cold.

The Wines Of Greece

Some travel-writers put undue emphasis on the resinated wines of Greece — the retsina — thus giving the impression that there is no other kind of wine to be had. This is not so. There is quite a variety of very good reasonably priced wines, red and white, dry or sweet, to suit all tastes — if one knows what to ask for.

Retsina is a wine flavoured with resin from the pine trees while still in the cask. It is extremely popular with the Greeks, particularly the *taverna* clientèle, and many visitors to Greece acquire a taste for it. On a hot summer's evening retsina mixed with soda water, as a long drink, can be very pleasing and refreshing.

Kokinelli is a rosé retsina and quite delicious.

Kampa is a very popular dry white wine.

Naoussa is a dry red wine.

Mantinea is a well-known and popular light wine from the Peloponnese.

Demesticha is a white and red table wine.

Zitsa is a wine similar to Champagne, from the Epirus region.

Mavrodaphni is a sweet dessert wine, which is highly recommended.

Castel Danielis is a dry red burgundy.

Château Decelie is very pleasant, and comes from the king's own vineyards.

Robola is a rosé wine from the Ionian islands.

Samos is a malmsey and muscatel wine. Byron wrote 'Fill high the bowl with Samian wine...' in praise of this distinctive wine.

Santorini is a potent wine with a distinctive flavour due to the volcanic soil of this island.

Commandaria is a wine similar to madeira from Cyprus.

King Minos is a very good golden wine from Crete.

Chevalier di Rhodi is a very pleasant red wine from the island of Rhodes. There are other regional wines, which though less well known are equally delicious.

Index of Recipes